Praise for *The G...*

"Too often, our imagination for what counts as su...
formed by capitalism than by the kingdom of God. In *The Gift of Small*, Allen Stanton offers a corrective, shifting our focus away from the distractions of average Sunday attendance to the making of disciples within context-specific missions. Stanton not only encourages smaller congregations—he celebrates them. Every word of this book is rooted in deep love of small congregations and the members that make them up. This book will help pastors, denominational leaders, and congregants grow in appreciation for the particular ways that they grow in shared spiritual life and share the gospel, both within their congregation and into the communities beyond."

—**Dr. Kate Rae Davis**, executive director, Center for
Transforming Engagement at The Seattle
School of Theology and Psychology, and
executive editor, *Christ & Cascadia*

"Allen Stanton illuminates the many gifts and abilities of small-membership congregations. He identifies leadership practices and key roles for clergy and laity who desire to see the small church exhibit health and vitality. Stanton calls us to see the small church as a community in which transforming discipleship can happen."

—**Bishop Tom Berlin**, Florida Conference, United Methodist
Church, and author of *The Third Day* and *Reckless Love*

"A strong sense of vocation is fundamental to a well-lived life. In this important work, Allen Stanton clearly demonstrates the ways in which personal and congregational vocation are uniquely interwoven in the small church and made manifest in the local community."

—**Rev. Phillip Blackburn**, director, Thriving in
Rural Ministry, University of the Ozarks

"Allen Stanton offers an impressive, refreshing, and uniquely multidisciplinary account. Drawing widely from theology, economics, sociology, political science, and ethics, Stanton fiercely advocates for small-membership congregations. *The Gift of Small* is essential reading for those leading and serving in and alongside small-membership congregations."

—**Laceye C. Warner**, Royce and Jane Reynolds Professor of the Practice of Evangelism and Methodist Studies, and associate dean for Wesleyan Engagement, Duke University Divinity School

The Gift of Small

The Gift of
SMALL

Embracing Your
Church's Vocation

Allen T. Stanton

FORTRESS PRESS
MINNEAPOLIS

THE GIFT OF SMALL
Embracing Your Church's Vocation

29 28 27 26 25 24   1 2 3 4 5 6 7 8 9

Library of Congress Cataloging-in-Publication Data

Names: Stanton, Allen T., author.
Title: The gift of small : embracing your church's vocation / Allen T. Stanton.
Description: Minneapolis : Fortress Press, [2024]
Identifiers: LCCN 2024013415 (print) | LCCN 2024013416 (ebook) | ISBN 9781506481937 (print) | ISBN 9781506481944 (ebook)
Subjects: LCSH: Small churches.
Classification: LCC BV637.8 .S73 2024 (print) | LCC BV637.8 (ebook) | DDC 254--dc23/eng/20240528
LC record available at https://lccn.loc.gov/2024013415
LC ebook record available at https://lccn.loc.gov/2024013416

Cover design and illustration: Kristin Miller

Print ISBN: 978-1-5064-8193-7
eBook ISBN: 978-1-5064-8194-4

To my sister, Laura.

Contents

Contents

Foreword

Small churches are an anomaly wrapped in an enigma, surrounded by paradox. They are everywhere (over 90 percent of churches are considered small), but they often go unnoticed. They come in an amazing array of shapes, styles, and types, but they're usually stereotyped by the little white chapel. They are a prime factor in driving the growth of the global church, yet the small church is often considered stuck or broken merely because it is small.

Big churches do some things better than small churches, while small churches do some things better than big churches. Small churches give more money per capita than big churches, but they often have trouble paying a full-time pastor's salary. They do more training and discipling of future pastors than big churches, but those ministers are more likely to serve on the staff of a big church. Small churches have a higher number of volunteers, but they are often under-trained.

Big churches are a blessing. Small churches are a gift. They're a gift to the people who worship and fellowship in them. They're a gift to the neighborhoods where they minister. They're a gift to the pastors who serve in them. And they're a gift, not in *spite* of being small but *because* they are small. The body of Christ is an astonishingly diverse group. And nowhere is that diversity seen and celebrated more than in the plethora of small churches from every culture, nation, language, neighborhood, and tradition imaginable.

If you pastor a small church, you have no doubt felt the guilt-inducing demands to get bigger to be considered successful. But striving for bigger is not the best way for small churches to serve the body of Christ. It's much better to understand what they offer at the size they are right now. That's how to leverage the gifts of the small church for the glory of God.

I encourage you to approach this book with open eyes and an open heart. Get ready to see small churches in a way you may not have considered before. Allen T. Stanton takes an honest, hopeful look at the gifts, challenges, and mission of the small church. So, like any gift, get ready to open it and be encouraged and delighted by what you find.

—Karl Vaters

Acknowledgments

This particular book came about during a weird part of my life. When I began thinking about what I wanted to write, the world was in the early days of the COVID-19 pandemic. My wife was pregnant with our second child. We were working from home on lockdown with a three-year-old daughter. Suffice to say, a lot was going on.

When I began writing the book, I was slowed down by a few things. First was the birth of a second daughter. At the same time, my job changed substantially when the small, private Methodist College where I was working was acquired by a public university system. As a result, I moved deeper into rural public policy, and my family relocated to Memphis, Tennessee, for our new jobs. I also began working with more cohorts of church pastors. I found kindred spirits with new friends and colleagues at the University of the Ozarks as a consulting fellow for their initiative to support rural ministry. Meanwhile, my full-time work found me managing a significant public policy initiative in a college of dentistry.

I offer this backstory for a couple of reasons: First, to say that writing in the midst of these changes meant writing in fits and spurts with long delays in between. More than a few times, I thought about letting the project go completely. Second, as a reminder to myself that throughout this book, there were a number of people supporting it, whether they knew it or not. So, like any good acknowledgment page, I'm going to list as many of them as I can remember. There were many, many others I am sure that I have inadvertently left out.

Beth Gaede and Yvonne D. Hawkins both offered outstanding editorial support for this project. Beth skillfully guided me through the creation of the idea and outline of this project, pushing me to think deeply about what I wanted to say. In our first conversation, I admitted that I had no idea what I wanted to write, and I am more than grateful for her tolerance and encouragement as I put my thoughts in order. Yvonne inherited this project after Beth's retirement. It is not hyperbolic to say that this book would not exist without Yvonne. I gave her plenty of chances to walk away from it; she gave me one of my new favorite phrases: "Life is gonna life." She also provided excellent notes and comments, pushback and cheerleading, and the book is better for it. Beth helped me figure out what I wanted to say. Yvonne helped me say it.

Rebecka Cronin's dedication to the programs of my previous center allowed me time to focus on writing. She also became my wife's volleyball teammate and my daughters' favorite family friend. Our conversations and jokes added levity to some tough days. Meghan Killingsworth and Brad Smith allowed me to share their experiences of small-church leadership.

Phil Blackburn and the University of the Ozarks offered me an outlet for my theological work, welcoming me as a partner in their new initiatives. The members of our now three-year-long cohort have allowed me to test much of the research and materials on them. It is a joy to teach that cohort and an even bigger joy to learn from them. Courtney Bacon-Latina, John Arnold, Susan Arnold, Bill Seitz, and Blake Brinegar are excellent examples of small-church leaders, and this book reflects many of our discussions together. Thank you for letting me be a part of this group and for our annual cigar.

When I began working in a dental school, I wondered how my new colleagues would react to a pastor wandering among them. Dr. Jay Ragain, our dean, has been nothing but supportive of my dual work. By the time this book comes out, he will have retired. It has been an honor serving under him. Ken Tilashalski, our executive associate dean, has no idea what this book is about but is a constant supporter of my writing. Most of all, I'm grateful for the work that I do in the College of Dentistry (at the University of Tennessee Health Science Center), especially when it comes to applying the organizational theories that I discuss in this book. Working in a statewide program has given me a deeper insight into organizational structures and relational leadership.

Most importantly, I have to thank my family. I always think it's sappy to say something like, "I couldn't have completed this book without my wife." But as cliché as it sounds, it is true. I could not have written this book without my wife, Abby. On a practical level, she let me travel around without the kids to teach cohorts and do my day job. While I long ago learned that she would not read my drafts, she has been my largest supporter. She has listened to me talk through my book, celebrated when I finished a chapter, and let me be frustrated when I wasn't writing as fast as I wanted to be writing. More than that, she keeps me sane and grounded. Plus, she and I laugh a lot, and I enjoy that. My two daughters, Paige and Natalie, have reoriented my thinking on vocation. Truthfully, this book would have been finished a lot sooner had they not been in the picture. But I would not have all of my treasured memories at the Memphis Zoo, walks by the Mississippi River, hikes through the woods in Middle Tennessee, and the huge amounts of ice cream the three of us have consumed together over the past few years. It was a more-than-fair trade. My sister, Laura, to whom this book is dedicated, is a fierce and brave person; probably the bravest person I know. Our phone calls have kept me sane on long drives. She tolerates my playlists when we do hang out, lets me leave long and rambling voicemails on her phone, and doesn't complain when I ask her professional nursing opinion. I relish being her annoying little brother, even if I am fourteen hours away.

This book is not perfect, but it has been made better by all the people who have left their fingerprints on it. Imperfect as it is, I hope that it provides some help and encouragement to the many small-membership churches who are faithfully seeking to be disciples of Jesus Christ.

Introduction

I want to start with a (sometimes) unpopular opinion: I prefer small-membership churches. I grew up in a small church, which I credit for giving me an opportunity to take on leadership roles I am not sure I would have gotten elsewhere. I pastored a small-membership church, which I found to be deeply fulfilling and deeply formational. I cherished the interconnectedness of that congregation. As a clergy person serving outside of the local church, a great deal of my work is spent working with small-membership churches. Every church that I have opted to attend (outside of a two-year stint in college when I worked at a larger church) has been a small congregation.

I love small-membership churches. I find them, usually, to be a great living embodiment of the kingdom of God, not dissimilar to those early congregations in Acts. As we still adjust to the changing world post-pandemic, I am keenly aware of our need for connection and deep relationships. Even the way we talk about God is relational—God's relationship with God's self in the Trinity; God's relationship with us through Jesus Christ and the Holy Spirit; God bringing us into relationship with each other.

At the same time, I am often dismayed at the way small-membership churches are perceived and talked about. When I pastored a small-membership church, I found myself hyperfixated on growth, much to my own frustration. We would launch new outreach programs, reinvest in youth, try to diversify our worship experiences, toy with sermon series and styles, all in an effort to get new members. Much of this, I recognize now, was rooted in fear: Fear that I was not a competent pastor if my church wasn't growing. Fear that we would not be able to sustain ourselves without new members. Fear that we were failing our gospel mandate if new members weren't attending worship services.

None of these fears were unique to my congregation. I've had the opportunity to work with small-membership churches all over the United States, and those fears are largely repeated. In my work with one church, a parishioner pulled me aside to bluntly ask, "When are you going to tell us how to get new members, so that our church doesn't close?" The church I grew up in tried a whole host of growth techniques, and yet the average worship attendance hasn't changed much since I graduated from high school.

Faced with this constant fear, I wanted to understand its origin. What I found was a bevy of church leadership studies and denominational policies that largely made a few assumptions. They assumed that a church that wasn't growing wasn't faithful to its theological mission. The argument is that since we are called to evangelism, we are called to add members to our church.[1] But there's a disconnect in that. We are called to evangelism, but that evangelism is to the church universal—not my particular church. Some growing denominations even prioritize growing new churches, intentionally keeping their churches rather small but starting multiple congregations to nurture those within them. A deep evangelism requires us to look at the totality of the church, not just an individual congregation or even just one denomination.

The assumption that every church should be growing also lacks a rigorous engagement with community demographics and organizational capacities. I remember once talking to a group of midwestern churches in a denomination that was not my own. I mentioned a small church of sixty. "That's huge!" one of the participants exclaimed. "Our churches are fifteen or twenty." A reality of church growth is that most churches grow in places where there is a population boom. Even in cities, small-membership churches are subject to the whims of neighborhood population growth. The church in a trendy neighborhood in midtown will have seen a different growth than the ones in an old-money neighborhood, which will be different still than the congregation in a low-income neighborhood.

The focus on church growth also reacts to the decline in church participation across the board. If fewer people are attending small-membership churches, aren't those churches at a greater risk of closing? Well, that depends. But the reality is that most churches are small congregations. The assumption of numerical growth as good can problematize the overwhelming majority of congregations.

This book is a response, of sorts, to those fears. I argue that being a small-membership church can be a faithful, vital, and viable incarnation of the kingdom of God. Small congregations, I believe, have a great deal to teach the rest of the church about our task as a formational community.

The idea that the small-membership church is a formational community will appear quite a bit throughout the book, so it's worthwhile to pause here and define what I mean by this. At its core, it means that a community, in this case a small congregation, has a responsibility to instruct and nurture the discipleship of those who participate within it. As a result, the formational community is teaching both thought and practice, helping members form beliefs, ethics, and practices.

Discipleship formation is a bit like raising a child. There are moments, like a sermon or a Bible study, when there is clear instruction. Sometimes, I have to have a one-on-one conversation with my children, so that we can discuss what went wrong. But it is also filled with practices and lived examples. If I want my daughters to learn sharing or honesty, I have to create an environment where sharing and honesty is the norm. When we talk about instructing people how to live with gratitude or repentance or forgiveness, our congregational community must be an example of how that is practiced.

The theologian William Abraham has defined this formational work as evangelism; it is how people are initiated into the community of God's kingdom. For Abraham, this formational imagination happens through at least seven areas. While people start in one or two of these areas, as they grow in discipleship, they'll begin to inhabit more of them.

First, faith formation requires a community that will grow together, from which an individual will learn and to which they will contribute. Second, it requires one to understand and assent to some shared ideas, such as the incarnation of Christ and the Trinity. Third, formation requires a shared adherence to some ethical standards. The community of faith, and the individual joining that community, will not decide that stealing is good, or that greed is allowable. If the community is going to be formed morally, then there must be some basic understanding of where that morality is rooted and what it entails. Fourth, initiation into Christian community requires some assurance from the Holy Spirit. Fifth, members of the community will necessarily learn to articulate their particular spiritual gifts and talents. Sixth, members of the community understand that their gifts must be used to the benefit of the whole congregation and community, not just for themselves. Finally, this formational initiation requires taking up some spiritual disciplines, like reading Scripture, prayer, and sharing in community.[2]

In offering this as a means by which people are initiated into the Christian community, Abraham pivots evangelism away from simply attracting people to the church or gaining new members. Instead, initiation into the Christian community becomes a lifelong formational process, one in which a person is constantly being formed and reformed, always moving deeper in all of these habits.

Throughout this book, when I talk about the small church as formational or as a discipleship community, this is the pattern to which I am referring. I believe that being a formational community, teaching people to be disciples both within and without the walls of the church, is the primary and fundamental task of the church. At my most simplistic understanding of the church, I believe that if the church is not forming people to be disciples, it is not doing its job.

It is because of my belief in the necessity of being a formational community that I have a passion for the small-membership church. The small-membership church is an opportune environment for that work, both theologically and organizationally. The small-membership church is a deeply relational entity. While this can be overplayed, the relationality of these churches provides opportunities for us to live the practices and habits—the ethics—to which Jesus calls us. Their smallness and flat organizational structure also provide for a nimbleness and responsiveness to the needs of their parishioners and communities. Rather than failures, I believe that small congregations are laboratories of faith development. They can be sources of wisdom for what it means to do church well.

OFFERING A WHOLISTIC VIEW

This book explores the particular gifts of the small-membership church and encourages these congregations to embrace their vocations as formational communities. To do that, the book is divided into three parts, each focusing on a necessary component of the small-membership church's vocation. Part 1 first examines our fascination with growth, both in church and in our wider culture. Then, we turn to the organizational characteristics of the small-membership church. Here, I want to take a closer look at why these churches are well suited to the work of being the church, the importance of the relational aspects that I have highlighted already, and the adaptive capabilities of these small organizations.

Part 2 explores the people of the small-membership church. Namely, we look at the people who seek out a smaller, close-knit community. Likewise, we look at a standard trope surrounding small-membership churches: these congregations are aging and are therefore doomed to die. By paying attention to the demographics of these congregations, we instead find that small-membership churches can be vital expressions of God's kingdom.

In part 3, I address the work of the small congregation. Here, we explore two facets of these congregations' work. First, we look at the ways people engage with small congregations, which is rather different from the ways they might engage with a larger congregation.

Second, we explore one of the most important ways that smaller congregations can be in ministry, helping members across generations to discover and rediscover their vocations.

In the conclusion, I argue that we need to reframe our conceptual images of what makes a vibrant church. I offer both biblical imagery and examples of two churches to aid in that work. Reframing what we picture as a healthy and vital church is imperative if we are to help small congregations embrace their gifts and fulfill their unique vocation.

I decided to structure the book into these three parts for a few reasons. Primarily, I wanted to offer a holistic view of the small-membership church. Churches are multifaceted places. They are organizational structures, with organizational realities, so this book weaves in organizational theory and behavioral economics to help clarify why, functionally, small churches behave the way they do and how we might use those behaviors for meaningful practice. Congregations are also sociological entities, so this book explores some of the sociology of the small-membership church, attempting to understand who goes to these churches, why they attend them, and what that says about their future. But most importantly, churches are theological entities with theological practices. I attempt to articulate a theological practice for these small-membership churches and understand their organizational and sociological behaviors in light of theology.

Like my previous book, this book began out of both frustration and hope. I find that these are often intertwined. My frustration was what I saw as a general malignment of small-membership churches. My hope was that by diving deep into the realities of the small-membership church, I could provide something that helps leaders in small congregations use the natural gifts of their churches to rediscover the vocation of their congregations. And, along the way, I hope to dispel a few problematic myths of small-membership churches.

In writing this book, I have tried to keep three audiences in mind. First are the pastors of these churches and the denominational officials that support them. I hope that what they read here will help them articulate their own understanding of the gifts of their congregations.

Second are the laity of these churches, without which the small-membership church could not exist. Laity are the lifeblood of small congregations. Their leadership should not be overlooked, and I hope that they find support for their contributions here. Finally, I hope that this book will find its way into the hands of those who are preparing to lead small congregations. I hope that they will see the small-membership church as a place of vital ministry and find opportunities for service in these congregations.

AVOIDING ONE-SIZE-FITS-ALL

It is helpful to outline a few things that this book is not intended to do. At the outset, I want to be clear that this book is not a technical guidebook on how to lead small congregations. Leadership is always contextual, and while I hope that this can be a valuable resource for those leading small-membership churches, there are no step-by-step guides here. In my work with congregations, I have found that there really is no one-size-fits-all approach to leading a congregation. Rather, I want to emphasize the natural gifts and traits of small-membership churches and support leaders as they make sense of that in their congregation.

This book is also not an attempt to help churches add new members or new worshippers. Often, at the end of a presentation or lecture, I'll field a question along the lines of "How will this help my congregation grow?" I hope that it helps your congregation grow spiritually. I hope you find it as a resource to deepen your discipleship. I hope that it can help your congregation grow its impact in your community. But I also must be honest and say that I hope to displace average worship attendance as the most important barometer of vitality.

Third, I am not suggesting that small-membership churches should be exempt from any sort of accountability. In fact, I would argue the opposite. We need increased accountability within our churches. But the measurements we use to hold ourselves accountable must actually align with our end goal. My hope is that small congregations will find this book useful in setting their own standards of accountability rather than simply defaulting to something like average worship attendance.

Finally, I'm not making any sort of argument about large churches. Obviously, my preference is for small-membership churches. But that is just my preference. This book is not a critique of large congregations. While I will often critique the idea that larger churches are more faithful or more vital, that critique is not a suggestion that large congregations are problematic. I want to hold up the natural gifts and abilities of small congregations. From time to time, I might compare larger and smaller congregations as a point of comparison, but I have worked hard to ensure that these are not judgments upon large or small churches.

The small-membership church has an important role in our world. In a world that needs deeper connections between people, when the church universal works to find out how to navigate in an uncertain future, when resiliency becomes more important, the small-membership church has ample wisdom to offer. It is incumbent upon the small-membership church to discover its own vocation. My hope for these congregations is that they will relish their vocations so that they might be something truly great: a small-membership church dedicated to the work of God's kingdom.

PART ONE

Organization of a Small Church

CHAPTER ONE

Our Fascination with Growth

We are a people obsessed with growth, especially numerical growth. Bloggers and church leadership websites regularly publish lists of the fastest-growing congregations. Denominational leaders tout helping churches grow as their primary goals. Pastors boast to other pastors about how their churches are growing and their plans to kickstart growth. Later, when those pastors become burned out, they often say with exasperation, "We've tried everything we can, but we just can't grow."

Once, while touring an area of my state with a denominational regional official, the official pointed out a small church and said, "That church is successful. It's growing like crazy. The theology is terrible—not at all what we teach. But they're growing!" The official wondered aloud why pastors who were more aligned with our denominational teachings had overseen a declining congregation. The numerical growth seemed a consolation prize—if the church couldn't have their denomination's teachings and grow, at least it was adding new people.

Our fascination with growth is not unique to the church. Rather, it is an obsession that is engrained in our wider cultural psyche. We like growth in the stock market, growing profits, opportunities for professional growth (and the salaries that accompany them), bigger houses, large cars. Athletic teams fight for new record attendance levels, cramming more and more people into stadiums. Even the size of our TV sets seems to be an indication of a person's progress: Growth is good. Bigger is better.

Our fascination with size is an improper goal for the local church. In fact, unmitigated growth in size is not always a healthy goal for any organization. For congregations, the focus on increasing average attendance can be a deceptive indicator, diverting us from our theological aspirations.

INFLUENCES SATURATING OUR IMAGINATIONS

The goal of growing churches larger did not emerge on its own. Rather, our fascination with numerical growth is indicative of the places where our moral and theological imaginations are formed. Understanding why we equate growth with faithfulness requires us to examine why we believe that size is important in the first place.

Ideally, the theology that we profess shapes our worldview and the actions we take to implement that worldview. Scripture makes this clear. In the letter to the Romans, for instance, Paul encourages Christians in Rome to "be transformed by the renewing of [their] mind," shaping their worldview after the "will of God."[1] Paul asks the Roman Christians to let their beliefs influence how they live their lives. Their beliefs would influence how they participate in every part of society: how they participate in government, shop, work, their treatment of strangers, the way they help the poor, and the way they resolve conflicts. In short, Paul argues that Christians' beliefs would reshape their political, economic, and social practices. James offers a blunter assessment in his epistle, writing that "faith by itself, if it has no works, is dead."[2] In short, James tells us, if our faith is not reflected in our day-to-day actions, if we are not being transformed in the way that Paul insisted, then our faith is worthless.

It is not a controversial statement to say that our theology is meant to shape how we understand and interact with the world around us. Allowing those beliefs to become formational is a pivotal component of becoming a Christian disciple. When we become people of faith, we join an "intellectual heritage."[3] The cognitive dimension of our faith, combined with the spiritual, shapes our morality and ethics.[4] If we are to be formed as disciples, then there is both the intellectual assent to the beliefs of the faith and a decision to put those beliefs into practice.

Church spaces, though, are not the only places in which we reside. Most people, even clergy, do not spend their days only reflecting on their theological beliefs. We spend our time in all sorts of contexts outside the walls of the church. It is unrealistic to expect that the sort of formation that the theologian William Abraham supposes only flows from the church to interaction in the world. While our theological beliefs shape how we view and engage the world around us, the world also shapes our beliefs. Our contexts, whether we are aware of them or not, also influence our moral imaginations. The actions in which we participate, and spaces where we perform those actions, will necessarily influence what we believe about the world and how we respond: how we think and act.[5]

Even something as simple as when we arrive somewhere helps us see how the world shapes our actions. In my first job out of seminary, I worked in a university think tank. My offer letter noted that the workday began at 9:00 a.m. and ended at 5:00 p.m. During my orientation, my supervisor pointed out that most people arrive by 8:30 a.m. Wanting to be a good employee, I arrived dutifully a half hour early like almost all of my colleagues. In my mind, being a good worker meant arriving early because my work environment formed my moral imagination to render early arrival as good.

Even after I became the single pastor of a small church, my habit was to arrive at the office a half hour before my workday officially began. I did this even though I set my own office hours. It was a habit I kept until I moved to my previous role. In our new town, it was my responsibility to take my daughter to daycare in the mornings. Officially, the workday began at 8:00 a.m. My daughter's daycare, though, did not open until 7:30 a.m., and it was a thirty-minute round-trip drive from my house. I could not both take my daughter to preschool and arrive at work thirty minutes early. Here, my family life and the time I spent in my home shaped my moral imagination. To be a good father meant taking care of my daughter. Being a good husband meant sharing the parental workload. These overruled my previous sensibilities and shifted my imagination of what it meant to be a good worker.

In both instances, the places where I spent my time, the culture of the space, and my understanding of the role shaped what I believed and how I imagined its virtue. Importantly, these identities, like employee, husband, father, are not independent. Rather, when they were in conflict with one another, my moral imagination negotiated to accommodate what it meant to be a good father and a good employee. I would go in to work on time rather than early because I needed to be a good father. I would take her when her preschool opened because a good employee is not late for work.

This is true theologically, but it is also true sociologically. Our experiences, or our social situation, create a worldview. That worldview becomes a way for us to interpret the world around us and helps us to decide what actions to take.[6] In her book *Worlds Apart: Poverty and Politics in Rural America,* the sociologist Cynthia M. Duncan reminds readers that our community relationships will shape our future goals. A child in poverty, surrounded by people who have never attended college, will most likely not attend college. The child never decided that they didn't want to attend college. Instead, they simply cannot imagine it. It is not in their sociological imagination.[7] When I arrived in college, I was surprised when a professor of mine suggested I consider a career as a Foreign Service Officer with the State Department. While I was vaguely aware that someone, somewhere must hold a job with those functions, I had never considered that it was a career choice open to me. I wasn't even sure how someone got those jobs. Later, when I discerned a call to ministry, I remember having a similar cognitive dissonance. I grew up in a different denomination than the one in which I wanted to be ordained. I remember feeling lost at the start of the process, totally unsure of how anyone actually became a United Methodist pastor.

One of the defining cultural lenses that influences our moral imagination is our economic worldview. Truthfully, economics is one of the largest, if not the single largest socially formational contexts in which we participate. The way that an economy performs can elect (or reelect) presidents. It instructs the kind of jobs we take, can put us at ease or cause anxiety—even when we go on vacation. At a basic level, the economy shapes our imagination through its ability to provide for our needs. I need to have a place to live, and I need to provide food and clothing for my family. Those of us who are fortunate to have more than enough to supply the basics imagine our needs in increasingly more complex ways: I need a larger vehicle, I need a home with a yard, I need a fast Wi-Fi connection, I need to afford a certain level of daycare for my toddler. Our economic worldview often guides our determinations about what is and is not important and necessary to us.

It is no surprise, then, that our views of economic life can shape, broaden, or limit our theological imagination. When we imagine the economy, we presume certain realities. People go to work, collect a paycheck, and use that paycheck on various goods and services. They pay their mortgage or rent, buy groceries, and spend some money on things they enjoy. Much of this we accept without question. No one seriously imagines an economy where you can earn large sums of money without any work at all (short of winning the lottery). Neither do we question that goods such as clothes cost money. Those are the economic facts to which we've adhered.

Theologians who think about economics and sociology largely assume the same basic principles. Some theologians will support our current economic systems as is, others will critique it or seek to modify the ways in which our societal understanding of economics is employed. As the theologian and ethicist D. Stephen Long illustrates, even thinkers who seek to dispose of capitalism begin by affirming its foundational presence in our worldview.[8] The basics of our existing economic system are ingrained in our imaginations. Beginning with that framework, the prevailing goal is trying to understand how to flourish on an individual and communal level.[9]

If we were to envision what economic flourishing would look like, we might use terms like *prosperity* or *wealth* to describe what we mean. To flourish in the economy is to do well. To do well is to continually be gaining—new income, new savings, more security. This is why in elections, campaigns appeal to our sense of well-being by referencing stock market growth and job growth. There is a societal presumption that the natural and good state of being is to continuously grow.

The field of economics, though, has not always presumed such perpetual growth. In charting the history of the field, the economist Kate Raworth points out that Aristotle distinguished between two terms, *economics* and *chrematistics*. The former focused on management of a household, while the latter was the "art of acquiring wealth."[10] Later, in 1767, the field of economics shifted to focus on ensuring that everyone had enough on which to survive, stable jobs, in a mutually beneficial society. Economist Adam Smith, whose ideas are the foundation of our modern economic system, had a similar goal, wherein individuals were able to provide for themselves, serve the community well, and where the state could enact public services. In these definitions, a balanced economy seems to be the goal.

Eventually, these ideas were merged with the philosophy of political economist John Stuart Mill, who began arguing that economics was about producing and accumulating wealth. Production and accumulation became the dominant way of understanding the political economy.[11]

In our economic imagination, increasing our societal and individual wealth is paramount. As a nation, we calculate this through the gross domestic product (GDP), and politicians argue that the more the GDP grows, the better we are. If the economy is not expanding, then we are dying. Political campaigns are waged on this premise; elections are fought, won, and lost over our GDP.

Growth is certainly not bad, but as Raworth reminds us, unmitigated growth can be disastrous. In any given environment, there needs to be a mutually beneficial balance, defined by a common goal. In a human body, for instance, the goal is to live. Cells must multiply, but only enough to maintain balance. Cells that multiply without any restriction, or too rapidly, will kill the body. Cells that multiply endlessly are quite literally cancerous. An overactive immune system, meanwhile, will begin to turn on and attack the rest of the body, making it sick. The same is true of any natural ecosystem. A river might be necessary to sustain life. If it has too much water, it can create a deadly flood. An overactive predator will destabilize the food chain, but an overabundance of their prey will also destabilize it. These ecosystems depend on a natural balance, with a natural goal to provide a habitat supportive of life.

Raworth's point is that our economic goals have long been centered on expansion. She argues that this is true because the images of our economics are pictures of growth—charts with lines that push upward and onward.[12] This perception of "all growth is good growth," has become a moral maxim of sorts. We participate readily and necessarily in the marketplace, we strive to be good employees and good citizens, and we yearn for stability and comfort. Our cultural realities, particularly our economic imagination, have given us an image that expansion is the appropriate avenue to achieve that.

When we arrive at church, we do not lose that imagination. In fact, as Senior and Long have both reminded us, it permeates the ways in which we think about what it means to be a successful church. It's no surprise then that vitality in the church is deeply related to "growth." When I became a pastor, our small congregation added a few new members with a slight bump in average worship attendance. Our sign in front of the congregation boasted, "We are growing!" The sign was, I think, an attempt to project that we were a healthy congregation, that we had potential. Underneath that was a presumption that the best way to live into that potential was to attract even more growth.

If adding new members is the key to being a successful congregation, then large churches are the most successful. Small-membership churches might not be viewed as failures, but they are certainly not exemplars of success. Assuming that more members means a healthier congregation is an assumption that is baptized with a weak theology. One goal of the church, and certainly a goal of evangelism, is to reach those who are not following Jesus Christ. The natural assumption is that a church with increasing membership is doing that more effectively. A small congregation, meanwhile, is not doing that effectively, because they are not recruiting new disciples. Growth, because it is the primary indicator, morphs into the goal. The question that churches need to ask is whether that is an appropriate goal at all.

FINDING A DIFFERENT *TELOS*

Much of our confusion about what makes a vital or strong congregation is because indicators of success—those things that we measure—have been conflated with our end goal, or *telos*. The shift from measuring our progress toward our goal to the measurement *as* the goal is an easy one to make. We begin with a simple goal (we want to share the good news of the gospel). We opt for a way to measure how effectively we do that (we want to invite people to church). Because sharing the good news of the gospel is hard to quantify, we report on our success in terms of what we are measuring. Over time, we lose sight of the original goal and focus on the measurement itself. Eventually, the only thing we care about is how we're measuring ourselves. Therefore, the measurement often defaults to assessing how many people are coming through our church doors.

This assumed connection between more people and success is a difficult one to break. The center I previously managed ran a cohort program where we work with rural pastors on leading community development initiatives. During one of the sessions, we would spend time talking about their initiative's goals and how they would measure success. Pastors routinely prioritized attendance, assuming a higher turnout would mean a successful event. One pastor shared that their goal was to increase knowledge of preventive care practices. The coach guiding this pastor in the planning process asked how they would measure progress toward that.

"We're aiming to have fifty people attend," came the response.

"But why?"

"Because then fifty people would have learned about preventive care practices."

The pastor's logic wasn't hard to follow. If the congregation wanted to share knowledge and practices that might make the community better, they needed to attract more people to make use of the practices. Nowhere in that line of thinking, though, was any evaluation of the quality of the information being taught, how well people retained it, and how likely they were to successfully implement the new knowledge. It was assumed that increasing the amount of people who attended would increase their progress toward a goal. In reality, having fewer people who more readily comprehended and utilized the knowledge would be of far more service.

Many small-membership churches have derided themselves because of the same faulty logic. Likewise, many small-membership churches would be more impactful by focusing on the smaller number of people with whom they interact. In order to determine whether that is true at all, though, we need to ask a much more basic question: What is our telos? What is the goal of the local church?

To answer that, the evangelist Mortimer Arias points to the Great Commission. The instructions from Christ are well known:

And Jesus came and said to them, "All authority in heaven and on earth has been given to me. Go therefore and make disciples of all nations, baptizing them in the name of the Father and of the Son and of the Holy Spirit, and teaching them to obey everything that I have commanded you. And remember, I am with you always, to the end of the age."[13]

Arias noncontroversially points out that this commandment ought to be a "fundamental paradigm for the mission of the church."[14] Arias's contention, though, is that the telos to which this commandment points is slightly different from the way it is popularly interpreted.

At a cursory read, the key phrases "make disciples" and "baptizing them" seem directly related to a numeric value. Reasonably, one might assume that if a congregation isn't adding new members, then they are failing to adhere to Jesus's fundamental commandment. The flaw in that assumption is that it divorces the process of making disciples from the lifelong formational work on which Jesus insists. Such a reading of the text would result in a three-step faith process: Step one, make disciples. Step two, baptize them. Step three, teach them. But, as Arias reminds us, the language Matthew uses does not represent these as three steps. Rather, "baptizing" and "teaching" are used to describe aspects of forming disciples.[15] Making disciples is not step one of a longer process; it is the process of forming people to a life of faithfulness.

The instruction, "teaching them to obey all that I have commanded you," takes on a new importance, even as it is left out of pithy mission statements of denominations and local churches riffing on the Great Commission. As Arias notes, teaching people *all* that Jesus has taught is to both reenact the work of the gospel and help others reenact that work as well.[16]

This is a significantly different approach toward understanding the goal of the local church. The goal is not to simply increase the numbers of people who participate in the life of the local church. Neither is it to just increase the numbers of people who profess a belief. Rather, the goal of the church is to help people live into the "coming Rule of God," a kingdom illustrated through the words and works of Jesus in the Gospels.[17]

Arias is not alone in his interpretation of the Great Commission. The biblical scholar Mitzi J. Smith, in her edited volume on the Great Commission, points out that a narrow reading of what it means to teach renders readers "blinded or indifferent [to Matthew's] pervasive emphasis on incarnational justice and the integral relationship between incarnational justice and teaching."[18] In the same volume, theologian Anthony G. Reddie further emphasizes the necessity to expand our understanding of education, specifically for Black Americans. Education, he argues, must "be concerned with enabling black people to have a profound appreciation of love and self . . . by reminding black youth that God, in whose image they are created, loves them and desires all that is good for their continued existence."[19] Arias, Smith, and Reddie all embrace an essential truth of understanding the gospel—it must be a lived reality. For Smith and Arias, living out our Matthean commission requires a special attention to addressing injustice. For Reddie, the emphasis on teaching must empower individuals to embrace who they are created by God to be. If our primary mission as a church is to teach the gospel, then it must also recognize and confront our social realities. To put it another way, simply increasing the number of professions, worship attendance, or even baptisms is at best an incomplete effort on the part of the church's attempt to abide by Jesus's commandments.

The evangelism scholar Bryan Stone rearticulates this as a formational act. According to Stone, the church's purpose is "to be formed imaginatively by the Holy Spirit through core practices such as worship, forgiveness, hospitality, and economic sharing into a distinctive people in the world, a new social option, the body of Christ."[20] Teaching the gospel, in this view, requires that participants in church learn practices that shape not just the intellectual or theological perceptions of its members. Instead, it must shape the ways in which congregants interact with each other and the wider world.

Stone's argument is effectively one of Christian ethics, examining how our notions of discipleship formation are to shape our actions. Drawing upon the work of philosopher Alasdair MacIntyre, Stone is not presupposing that the church can simply offer a rationalized and exhaustive list of what to do and not to do in every situation. Rather, the church has a responsibility to cultivate a virtuous imagination so that its members can eventually and instinctively learn to practice what is right and good.

For MacIntyre, a virtue is a quality that "enables an individual to achieve [their telos] and the lack of which will frustrate his movement towards that telos."[21] A knife has a telos of being able to cut well. If it is dull and unable to cut, it has lost its progress toward its telos. The virtue that it needs is sharpness. MacIntyre insists that cultivating virtue and moving toward telos requires three foundational aspects. First, a person's telos is intimately tied to a broader narrative.[22] The story in which they participate will ultimately help point toward their end goal and the virtues they need to cultivate. Narrative also places a person within a larger historical context, removing the sort of individualism that pervades many ethical frameworks. Instead, a person is placed into a community with traditions. These traditions, in turn, teach us to respond to the world in helpful and unhelpful ways.[23] These traditions constitute the second component of MacIntyre's framework.

The final component is what MacIntyre refers to as a practice. For MacIntyre, practices are things that happen in communities, are challenging, are appreciated by the community, have standards of excellence, and can grow and strengthen over time.[24] Importantly, a routine task is not a practice. So, as MacIntyre describes it, "throwing a football with skill" is not a practice, "but the game of football is."[25] To be good at the practice of football, a player must not only know how to throw well, they must also be adept at reading the defense, knowing when to throw, when to scramble, how to avoid being hit, and when to throw the ball away. Over time, the standards of what constitutes good practice will evolve as players and coaches systematically respond to each other and strengthen their skills. The game of football retains many of the same elements as it did fifty years ago, but it is also noticeably different.

Narratives, traditions, and practices all interact to form the virtues that make it possible to reach a telos. Narratives and traditions will shape practices while practices will in turn shape the traditions by which we remember the narratives. Rather than become circular, though, they illuminate and help make sense of each other. Brad Kallenberg, a theologian who extensively relies on MacIntyre's philosophy, borrows the metaphor of a sunrise, where the light gradually illuminates the whole landscape.[26] Consider this simple example. As a United Methodist clergy person, I am required to attend a yearly event called Annual Conference. The multi-day event starts with a clergy session, where we largely take pro forma votes on procedural matters and approve the candidates for ordination. Each year during the clergy session, I sit at the back with a friend and mentor of mine. We catch up, crack jokes, and trade stories. We reminisce on previous Annual Conferences and plot out how we will spend our week.

There is a clear tradition here. Each year, my friend and I come together in a particular place at a particular time. There is a practice of friendship at work through conversation, remembering events, sharing, and jokes. Over the years, this has created a narrative. Some of that narrative is evidenced in the way the stories we share compound, self-referencing themselves with shorthand inside jokes about shared experiences. Some of that narrative is evidenced in the way that we articulate to others what is happening: this is a friendship and sitting together at this event is an important component of that. In turn, that narrative strengthens the tradition. I look forward to the clergy session because I know that I will hang out with my friend whom I don't often get to see. When I was finally able to attend Annual Conference in person after COVID, I told my wife that I was most looking forward to the clergy session because of this tradition. Subsequently, each practice of the tradition reinforces the narrative and adds to it. The practice of friendship is shared, and we add new stories to the broader narrative.

To adequately describe how important this event is to my friendship with this person requires articulating the tradition, narrative, and the practices at work. The practice of friendship helps explain why the tradition exists and gives meaning to the narrative of the friendship. The tradition helps explain the narrative and gives some context to the practice. The narrative helps make sense of the practice and the tradition. Like Da Vinci's self-supporting bridge, the narrative, tradition, and practices are interlocked and rely upon each other.

The telos of the church is life in the kingdom of God. Per the Great Commission, this happens as the church baptizes and teaches people. Arias starkly summarizes it like this: "Jesus had no other subject than the coming rule of God."[27] If this is the telos of the church, then Christians must be intentional about remembering the narrative, imparting the traditions, and taking up the practices of the community. The church is at its best, or in MacIntyrian language—at its most virtuous—when it is helping orient the community toward the kingdom of God.

The narrative and traditions are further learned through the peculiar practices that the church teaches. We learn about the hospitality of Christ when we practice hospitality. We learn about repentance from hearing of our roles in perpetuating pain in wider narratives. We learn about the forgiveness that Christ offers when we learn to forgive others. We learn about gratitude by practicing gratefulness. All of these are deeply personal practices, which require communal giving and receiving.

Consider hospitality, for instance. Contemporary culture has defined hospitality along the lines of making people feel welcome. At a larger church, hospitality might just mean feeling oriented within the church service or having someone show you around. This type of hospitality can easily be forgotten, though, as it is less concerned with deep and meaningful relationships. Similarly, this type of hospitality is often tied to an organizational ambition, such as attracting new members, rendering the virtue as less important than the goal of growth.[28]

The hospitality illustrated in the Gospels is far deeper, and far more difficult. It requires a level of comfort with being interrupted, an invitation into the messiness of our home or life, a vulnerability to show what might not be perfect, and accepting that someone might not respond in an anticipated way. Hospitality might even mean that someone takes advantage of generosity.[29] Most often, that sort of deep hospitality, which impacts both the giver and the receiver of the hospitality, takes place among a small number of people. We learn hospitality when a neighbor shows up needing to talk when our house is not clean. We learn hospitality when a child carrying a Palm branch on Palm Sunday deviates from the intended parade route and instead runs to their mother. Hospitality is learned in intimate settings rather than large ones.

The same could be said of many of the aforementioned practices. Repentance requires a personal connection, wherein the person repenting must acknowledge how their actions hurt another and how they can turn away from their action. This is more likely to happen in intimate moments, where we can share in the stories of a few, finding how our stories are all interconnected. We learn forgiveness when we are hurt, and yet we show up to the church dinner and eat with the member who has wronged us, knowing that we need each other more than we need our anger. We remember gratitude when we pass by the small plaques commemorating the donation of a long-deceased church member, and we remember and retell how their contribution and their life shaped us and the congregation to which we belong.

All of these require a deep knowledge about the community, the story, the traditions of the community, and about each other. They cannot happen in the isolation of a large crowd; they need relationships in order to take root, change us, and guide our practices outside of church. This in turn invites the question: if the depth of relationships is vital to the mission, the telos, of the church, should growth be the emphasis?

CLARIFYING NEW POSSIBILITIES

I am not at all arguing that those who advocate for numerical church growth believe that a large church is the ultimate telos of the church. The Church Growth Movement began and continues in an earnest desire to make new disciples.[30] Nonetheless, our fascination with increasing in size stems from the way we imagine success in our political and economic world. In turn, churches focus on growth that unintentionally overrides and obscures our vision of the different possibilities for vitality and the ways that churches might move toward their telos.

The result of this is that we assume a healthy church is a large and growing church and an unhealthy one is a small, stable church. We in the church need to rediscover our telos. That telos is to make disciples who are able to enact the kingdom of God in our lives as a community, both within and without the walls of the church.

Evangelism scholar Priscilla Pope-Levinson recounts a story told by Donald McGavran, the founder of the Church Growth Movement when McGavran met a pastor who decried the movement because of the preponderance of churches in the community. Later, when speaking to a group of pastors in the town, McGavran pointed out that in the community of 30,000, there were sixty-one churches accounting for less than 6,000 in average worship attendance. That meant, according to McGavern, there were 24,000 people who were not disciples. For McGavran, church growth was a way to reach those people.[31]

Here, the telos is still to create disciples by getting people into church. But McGavran's story is also laden with theological assumptions. The largest of these is the assumption that church attendance is synonymous with faithfulness to our biblical mandate to make disciples. It is true that faithfulness and discipleship require community. It is not true that everyone participating in that community will be faithful or pursue deeper avenues of faithfulness. Likewise, as Pope-Levinson highlights, McGavran's concern is not about what happens in the walls of the church, even as teaching is an essential component of the Great Commission. Rather, his concern is entirely rooted upon "who is *not* in church on a given Sunday."[32]

One of the largest questions raised by the Church Growth Movement is how those people are formed. By focusing largely upon who is not within the walls of the congregation, proponents of church growth risk perpetually punting the important work of formation. In fact, according to Pope-Levinson, discussion around the kingdom of God within the Church Growth Movement is oddly muted.[33]

When church size becomes the primary focus, it is easy to lose sight of the virtues necessary for the church to fulfill its telos. For instance, one of the tactics of church growth is creating homogeneous groups of people because people are generally more comfortable connecting to others who are like them.[34] The Church Growth Movement's insistence on homogeneity was connected to the larger social setting of the late 1960s and 1970s.

According to religious historian Jesse Curtis, one of Donald McGavran's key concerns in 1968 was his view that evangelism and social justice were distinct and opposed, and a fear that advocates for social justice would reduce an emphasis on evangelism.[35] Critics of the Church Growth Movement were vocal about their perception of racial injustice within the movement. Clarence Hilliard, copastor of the interracial Circle Church in Chicago, argued that the Church Growth Movement made Christianity into a transaction, severing a link between Christianity and the need for justice.[36] McGavran argued that after people became Christians in their homogeneous communities, they would pick up the social teachings of the gospel.[37] Yet, the community that McGavran's tactics form lack the practices, narratives, and traditions necessary to move toward a telos where justice is prioritized and embodied. How can a core value of the gospel like hospitality emerge from practices that are oppositional to the value itself?

Even for those who seek innovative ministry, adding new members to a congregation remains an irresistible metric. In his book *Canoeing the Mountain,* Tod Bolsinger, a prominent congregational strategist and professor, applies the theories of adaptive leadership to leadership within the church. Bolsinger uses the story of Meriweather Lewis and William Clark's westward expedition across the United States as a parable of adaptive thinking. One of the most compelling points comes when Bolsinger describes the adjustment that Lewis and Clark make when they realize that their initial goal was pointless. They set out to find the Northwest Passage and, upon realizing that it does not exist, they reframe their mission based on their chartered values.[38] In a culture that is becoming or is already post-Christian, Bolsinger argues that the church will need to reframe its task. Leaders should not be tempted by quick and easy answers, default to prior solutions, or seek out solutions that do not correspond to their core ideology, Bolsinger insists.[39]

The challenge in this is that Bolsinger is still tied to the desire to see the church increase in size. His fundamental question is, "What can we do to keep the church from dying?"[40] Per his own description, a dying institution is a church that is not growing.[41] Ironically, the commitment to this dominant metric runs counter to the adaptive leadership model that Bolsinger touts, wherein the default interpretations of a problem and their solutions must be continuously questioned.[42]

If the mission of the church is tied to the Great Commission and enacting God's kingdom, then whether a church is becoming larger tells us precious little about the church. It can tell us about how many people enjoy participating in that church, and, as Stone points out, it can even tell us that people are having some need—real or perceived—met within that church.[43] But, it cannot tell us if the church is helping a group of people learn the habits and virtues that Jesus commanded the church to teach or whether the kingdom of God is being enacted.

DEFAULTS OF THE SMALL CHURCH

There is another, more basic organizational reality to any given congregation. While we often imagine churches to be places of deep theological reflection or virtue, they are also complex organizations. They have staff members, volunteers, budgets, income, operational costs, and program expenses. Larger churches, necessarily, have more corporate structures. They have well-defined staff hierarchies and operational policies. Because of their structure, they have clearer and more rigid budgets, and more policies that govern human resources and staffing.

An unintentional side effect of larger organizations is that they become more bureaucratic and more reliant upon defined policy. When I was a seminary student at a major research institution, I worked as a graduate resident, meaning that I lived in and helped oversee an undergraduate dorm. Because it was a large university, there were strict guidelines in place around the types of programming allowed, who had to approve various programs, and how much flexibility existed. It typically took a few days to receive approval for a program or initiative. Programs that slightly aberrated from the standard policy required multiple levels of approval, which might take weeks to receive. All of that is necessary, of course, because if every dorm or group of students wanted to do something slightly outside of convention, the purpose and value of the programs would quickly become co-opted by competing interests seeking to use available resources. As a result, it is much more advantageous to stay within the system and produce results that align with whatever standards the system demands.

My previous institution was not a nationally known research institution but rather a small regional college that caters to rural students. Our organization was rather flat; my center constituted its own administrative department. While we lacked the funds of a major research institution, we also lacked the rigidity of those universities. Because I was my own administrative unit, the institution tolerated a fair number of new ideas. I could work with my staff to ideate and quickly run an experiment or a trial. Because each department is small, I easily found the decision maker in another area to discuss a collaborative idea. If I needed the president's signature on an idea, there was no challenge in scheduling a meeting and pitching something. Our resources may not have been endless, but we were able to maneuver quickly. As a result, there was a fair amount of interdepartmental collaboration.

The organizational structure will shape and form the culture of an institution, which in turn shapes and forms the ways people approach their work. If I know that collaboration will require navigating a complicated bureaucracy, then I will be less likely to exert the effort required to build meaningful collaborations. In turn, even if collaboration is a named value of the institution, it will not be prioritized. Just as our theological ideals can shape our organizational structures, the organizational structures can shape the theological virtues that we value.

This is similar to what economists Richard Thaler and Cass Sunstein call *choice architecture*. In the field of behavioral economics, it is understood that people make decisions that are not always logical. People are more likely to save for retirement if the funds are deducted before they receive their paycheck. Likewise, they are more likely to join their employer's retirement plan if they are required to opt out rather than requiring them to opt in.[44] As a rule, people tend to choose the default option available to them, whether it is in their best interest or not.[45] Organizations, then, must be cognizant of how they are designing the choices that people make.

How does this relate to a church? Imagine a church that talks frequently about hospitality. The pastor forms a welcoming team who designs a first-time visitor station. The team has greeters who say hello to people as they come in and who will even walk with someone to their car or carry an umbrella for them on a rainy day. The staff members encourage church members to join the hospitality team, reminding them that hospitality is one of their values. A number of people join the team, it becomes self-governing, and the pastoral staff no longer actively manage it.

There is a myriad of choice-design elements in this scenario. Church members are given a natural way to engage with newcomers and regular worshippers. For example, I once worked in a large church where I was also a member during my college years. I rarely attended a regular worship service because my job was to coordinate the children's worship services. Near the end of my seminary years, I returned for a visit. There was a new pastor and children's minister. Most of the staff had changed, so I knew almost no one.

When I arrived for the worship service, alone and in my twenties, the greeter took a few moments for casual conversation. I mentioned that I used to work there in college. They took me to sit near a family of one of the children who had gone through our program, someone that I would know. The system was designed in a way where my default option was to talk to a greeter, and the greeter's default was to ask certain questions, such as "Is this your first time here?" From there, we were able to make natural connections, and that facilitated an experience where I avoided sitting alone in a large sanctuary.

A downside to this system, though, is the risk of making participants complacent. Participants are only required to be hospitable when it is their turn, and no one is pushing them to ask what the next step in being more hospitable might be. The greeter system is welcoming, but it is not pushing anyone to build a new relationship, or to tolerate—or even welcome—the disruption that hospitality often brings to our lives. Ultimately, this type of system creates a default option for people to learn some attributes of hospitality but will simply perpetuate the basic practice with which it began.

As behavioral economists point out, people enter a system and tend to follow the default options presented to them. The architecture of the choice-making process and the defaults within it signals participants to what the norm is. Within a church, the default choice is even more powerful because it signals that the default is aligned with the mission of the church. As Thaler and Sunstein note, opting for the default choice "will be reinforced if the default option comes with some implicit or explicit suggestion that it represents the normal or even the recommended course of action."[46]

That our systems create certain default choices has important implications for the systems perpetuated by typical church growth tactics. First, if the message that people receive is that increased average worship attendance and virtue are intimately related, leaders and members of the church may lose sight of the telos of Christian formation and instead focus on tactics that might hamper the formation of certain virtues.

Second, as churches grow, their organizations also become more bureaucratic. Intentionally or unintentionally, those organizations will perpetuate theological ideas, calcifying the tactics and methods that produced them. If growth is what fuels the stability of the organization, it will be difficult for the institution to disaffiliate from that because it needs to survive.

Third, organizational structures become the architecture that influences our choices, meaning that our institutions influence how people engage with their faith. Since most people will opt for the default position, their formation will be in that which facilitates the organizational goal, whether that is properly oriented or not.

Church size primarily indicates that the organization has achieved a system that is capable of perpetuating numerical growth, might or might not be forming people to the goal of enacting the kingdom of God, and is adept at enabling people to make a default decision to participate in the organization. The size of the church does not indicate, though, whether the members of the community are being formed to enact the kingdom of God in their day-to-day lives. In order to gauge the efficacy of that spiritual formation, one needs to look at the default choices the organization is allowing.

The sort of virtuous formation that Bryan Stone and Alasdair MacIntyre describe necessarily happens within community. But virtuous formation is not guaranteed to happen, though, unless it is habituated into the institutional and organizational life of the community. The narrative, traditions, and practices described by MacIntyre must be interpreted by the community, but the church must also be formed by those things. The type of formation advocated for here, which is oriented toward enacting the reign of God, is a "form of life" that cannot "exist without institutional forms."[47]

While Stone is correct to point out that there is no one institutional form, certain traits seem to foster virtuous formation. Traits can play different roles in an institution, depending on the default organizational systems at work. In my work, I have found four traits in particular that play an outsized role in the organization and formation of small-membership churches. To start, virtuous formation requires a deep sense of community, going beyond the basic act of belonging to the same congregation. As ethicist Christine Pohl points out, the communities we often inadvertently create "is community on our terms, with easy entrances and exits, lots of choice and support, and minimal responsibilities."[48] The type of community that can help members learn the traditions and habits of faithfulness requires much more vulnerability, which can be awkward and messy. Sharing a prayer request with a stranger in the pew can be intimidating, even if you belong to the same congregation. However, a community that builds trust, in turn, can both allow for vulnerability and create a space to learn the habits of the church.

Next, there must be leadership that mentors other generations and prepares them to lead. Small-membership churches are well-equipped to do this because, as we will see in the next chapter, small-membership churches are organized through their relationships. One of the primary organizational realities of a small congregation is that members know one another. The small-membership church creates a social fabric where each member can be located.[49]

This familiarity is particularly useful when forming intergenerational relationships. An older adult and a teenager or young adult are not forging a new relationship but relating to a person they know in a new way. Growing up in a small-membership church, my parents and I were always known in relationship to my grandmother. When I became a teenager looking for leadership roles in the community, the church was a natural place to look. Because I was Jean's grandson, older members would take me under their wing, teaching me how to play instruments, run sound equipment, and help with church finances. The relational nature of the church ensured that I was part of a network. Mentoring became a natural extension of that network rather than requiring that I build an entirely new one.

The third organizational attribute that the formational community needs, and that is native to small congregations, is a sense of story. This narrative will help shape the practices. In turn, it will also set the trajectory for what is to come. For established small-membership churches, the story is easily recognizable. A communal story is not unique to a small-membership church, though it is understood in a different way. In organizational studies, the guiding narrative is referred to as a canonical story, or a community narrative. Stories tell the members of the organization something about themselves, and it is reinforced in myriad ways: pictures, oral traditions, social rituals, and written documents.[50] These are different from a dominant cultural narrative, which is overlaid on a larger culture—for instance the difference between a neighborhood and the rest of a city, or between a town and the wider nature. Community stories are shared by members; dominant cultural narratives are communicated through shorthand stereotypes, like when we describe "kids these days" or say "OK, boomer."[51]

As we will see later in this chapter and throughout the book, small-membership churches are substantially different organizations than other institutions. Inside a larger institution, there are many smaller communities that exist, while smaller congregations are typically composed of a singular relational body. The sociologist Carl Dudley describes these as relational cells. In a larger congregation, there are multiple access points for an individual to enter the community. In a small-membership church, there is just one cell, the relational cell of the congregation.[52] We see this pattern replicated in other organizations. For instance, in my current university, there are multiple colleges. While we have the same dominant narratives (which are visible in our branding and repeated in our strategic plan), each college has its own distinctive cultural narrative. In my previous institution, which was significantly smaller, departments were less rigid, and by virtue of their frequent interaction, shared the same community cultural story.

In a small-membership church, individuals are more likely to share in a similar community cultural narrative because there is no other community group than the whole congregation. Learning the community narrative is part of the initiation into the congregation. In my previous pastorate, even newer members could retell the history of the congregation and the thought process behind key decisions. It is shared in formal and informal spaces. For instance, every year my church had a spring fundraiser, a pulled-pork barbecue dinner. When we would chop the barbecue, one of the older members would invariably begin to tell part of the story. "Pastor, did you ever hear about the elephants at the railroad?" The story was only nominally about elephants—a rumor that one time an elephant had been used to load railway cars at a station that used to be nearby, the remnants of which are now under a lake. The larger narrative, of course, was about how the lake had changed the community, and how the church had renegotiated their own values and identity based on that. Decisions about our next steps were made with those stories in mind: are we repeating a mistake of the past? Are we holding fast to a foundational value that is essential to who we are?

Newer small congregations will have a formational story in which new members are initiated. They will have a story of what drove people to that small group, the struggles of beginning, and the values that keep them focused. While the story will be shorter, it is no less important. It too is passed on to new members during their initiation into the community, framed within a reminder about who the community is and where it is going.

The final attribute is the ability of all members to share in stewarding the resources of the community. Through this, members of the community can learn the particular social and economic habits of the Christian community. A small-membership church has more accessibility to information about the budget process because small operations need support from all of the members.[53] In my first pastorate, the church council reviewed the finances every month. The church council consisted of around fifteen people, roughly a quarter of our average worship attendance. This really meant that practically every family unit in the congregation had at least some representation on the council.

The flattened hierarchy also meant that discussions about our resources felt more real. If we were a few thousand dollars under budget, it meant one of the families in that room would be helping to offset that deficit. Because there was a face associated with each dollar given, we had a deep respect for how we spent our money. It was often unspoken, but our stewardship needed to honor the sacrifices of the members who gave. At times, this can morph into something unhealthy. An upset member might threaten to withhold their money or gifts if they don't get their way. And, since each person's offering is needed to sustain the church, this can be a crippling and abusive action.

Done well, though, this deeply personal way of relating to a fairly mundane document can help us better picture the economics of the kingdom of God, whereby we are invited into the household of God, where all gifts are given to God's glory. As such, this sort of economic practice reminds members that all are invited to participate, and that participation "subverts rival ideological claims about family, gender, race, sexuality, or class."[54]

My first pastorate was home to members across the economic and class spectrum. Some were highly educated with incomes to match; others were struggling to pay their rent. One older lady consistently gave a small amount to the church, while scraping by each month on a small retirement income. One summer, she was scammed out of a substantial amount of money while trying to help someone. She lost her meager savings and found herself in a small amount of debt. Upon finding out what had happened, other members of the church quietly paid off her debt and ensured that she had enough to cover her needs. As one parishioner told me, "She has almost no money to her name, but has always given her twenty-dollar check each month. She did her best to take care of this church, and now it's the church's turn to take care of her." Our intimate nature as a small church, where each gift is valued, formed our imaginations about the economics of what it means to be a Christian community.

To reiterate, I am not suggesting that the four attributes described above are only found in the small-membership church. But while they may be found elsewhere, they are the building block of the default choices available to the small-membership church. They are the intrinsic traits that a smaller congregation will be organized around, whether recognized explicitly or not.

A great danger for the small-membership church is that the small church might attempt, to borrow again from Raworth, to overgrow. A church that wants to grow beyond its relational, solitary cell will necessarily move into multiple cells. As a church grows, it will need to reevaluate how it understands its organizational identity and strengths. A growing church will eventually be required to move beyond its relational leadership.[55] A church that is constantly growing will eventually cease to be a small-membership church, which means that it cannot rely on the same attributes and assets it had as a small organization.[56]

Not every congregation needs to be consistently adding new members or participants, though. Small-membership churches have enormous attributes, and they do not need to grow beyond themselves to be vital, formational communities. Rather than seeking to constantly outgrow themselves, they can learn to celebrate that they are already places with important natural gifts. If the mission of the church is to enact the kingdom of God, then the small-membership church is perfectly positioned to be a place of deep theological, ethical, and social formation. They are already big enough for the mission.

CHAPTER TWO

Relational Leadership

In my denomination, pastors are appointed to parishes. Time after time, I hear a theme from those who make appointments to those who are being appointed to their small congregations: this is a church that just needs someone to love them. Embedded deep into the psyches of many small-church pastors is an idea that pastoral leadership in these settings is primarily a chaplaincy service. Small churches, says conventional wisdom, are not going to be active. Rather, they need a pastor who primarily will care about them.

Theologian Will Willimon quotes ethicist Stanley Hauerwas as saying that modern clergy are little more than a "quivering mass of availability."[1] Willimon uses Hauerwas's critique to describe a ministry that is primarily focused on meeting individualized needs, prioritizing a therapeutic role for the pastor, and diminishing other leadership work.[2] This individualistic focus undercuts the true ministry of the pastor, Willimon argues, which entails far more than providing a counseling service. Rather, Willimon has argued, pastoral leadership is about bringing churches into mission and vitality. It is about *doing*, not just *being available*.

Cary Nieuwhof, a church growth blogger and podcaster, critiques relationship-focused leadership even further. Nieuwhof advocates that a successful church is one that is growing larger. Nieuwhof juxtaposes pastors who have no interest in increasing the sizes of their congregations to those who "want to see their mission fully realized."[3] If a church is going to grow larger, then a pastor must stop offering a personal relationship to every congregation member, Nieuwhof argues. Otherwise, Nieuwhof asserts, a congregation will settle at a maximum of a hundred people. Nieuwhof correlates growth with church size and sees a church that is growing larger as distinctive from a stagnant church. A church that is growing larger is one in which "God change[s] lives."[4]

Nieuwhof takes a more extreme position than Willimon, but both find some amount of fault in a congregation that is overly reliant upon relationship-building as the dominant focus of the pastor. This position takes issue with that of congregational studies researcher Carl Dudley, who offers a description of the "lover" pastor, known personally by all the congregation's members. According to Nieuwhof's and Willimon's thinking, if leadership in a small-membership church is going to be focused on developing relationships, then it is not going to be focused on growth in attendance, mission, programs, or other tasks that make the church vital and successful. The solution is to behave like a large church. For Nieuwhof, that means shifting the pastoral care responsibility to others while the pastor focuses on developing new organizational systems. In this view, the overemphasized role of relationships is a challenge to be overcome, not a natural component of the church.

However, relationships are an essential component of the small-membership church. Small-membership churches, as Dudley notes, are built around relationships. Dudley describes small churches as caring cells where "human relationships are primary."[5]

Because of their relational focus, a small church requires a pastor who is predisposed as a lover pastor. Here, the pastors are embedded into the relationships of the congregation so that they are actually available—not as a professional in service, but as a real person with whom all of the congregation can share a meaningful personal relationship.[6] According to Dudley, the lover does not need "constant and consistent measurement of achievements" but rather should be someone who "finds rewards in relationships with people."[7] While this type of leadership could be dismissed as Willimon and Hauerwas's "quivering mass of availability," it instead should be viewed as important for the leadership of the small-membership church.

Relationships are complex. In any system, there are toxic personalities. Cliques and groups can dominate discussions. But there are also moments of great beauty and communal support. The relationships of a small-membership church can be remarkably helpful, allowing quick and frequent communication, exchange of new ideas without cumbersome hierarchies, and strong bonds to form that carry people and the institution through difficult moments. We might be tempted to view a focus on relationship-building as defaulting to a ministry of availability. The reality of the small church, though, is that the action of ministry happens through relationality rather than in spite of it. In turn, relational leadership provides the foundation for healthier discipleship formation.

SOCIAL FABRIC AND DECISION-MAKING

Daniel Kahneman, one of the founders of behavioral economics, argues that human beings are not always rational. To be always rational, he notes, is to always be logically consistent, never swayed by emotional appeals, outside influences, temptations, or pressures.[8] This is a far cry from the standard economic models that predict human behaviors, which insist that decisions are made in a vacuum. In those models, people buy groceries based on how much money they can spend and what meals they're planning to eat. Such a model is cold and infallibly rational. But people, Kahneman insists, are not. We know that hungry shoppers will buy more food, and that items at eye level are more likely to be bought than those near the floor. We are influenced by a huge array of factors, some of which we are cognizant, many of which we are not.[9] While people are often thoughtful—a point with which Kahneman agrees—they are not always rational.

This was a particularly bitter pill for me to swallow when I began pastoring my first church. I have long loved data, spreadsheets, and well-crafted arguments. My favorite professor in college banned the phrase "I feel" in his classroom. He was insistent that within the classroom, we only think, not feel. I appreciated the cold, logical analysis of his coursework.

When I arrived at my small church, I thought that I needed to make a clear strategic plan for the congregation. I got to work finding ways to collect data. I did a survey with carefully worded questions and a variety of response types. I held listening sessions around different themes so I could get a sense of what topics kept coming up. I went to coffees, lunches, and dinners with people of different age groups, people who had recently joined, people from the area, and those who had just moved in.

Along the way, I realized that there was a small storage closet next to my office. The copier was down the hall in the choir room. I thought we could both clean up the storage room, make space for the choir, and move the printer closer to my office. After all, I was printing and copying a lot of stuff. While we were cleaning up the storage room, someone mentioned in passing that the room used to be a children's Sunday school classroom. We went back to talking about the surveys, listening sessions, and what I was learning about the church.

Once we had finished the data collection, I took my leadership council off for a half-day planning retreat. We passed out the surveys and listening session notes, and I began going over the results. I was thrilled that our strategic planning would be rooted in something rational, based on some pretty decent datasets.

To my dismay, the conversation was derailed fairly quickly. Buried in one of the open-ended answers was a criticism of a church tradition that was important to a few of the leadership council members. I insisted that we were not making any decisions based on one response and that it wasn't personal. Still, the conversation stalled as we read through the survey. The group tended to ignore the positive attributes of the survey and instead focused on the critiques, which were all taken as personal judgments on their work.

Later in the day, our conversation turned toward the children's ministry. At the time, most of our under-eighteen population were in the youth group, and so we began talking about how to strengthen that part of our church. In the conversation, someone expressed dismay that we had turned a classroom into a work room. "We made that room into a copier room. It said to me that we just don't care about the kids," the person said.

A few others murmured their agreement. I pointed out that the room hadn't been used as a Sunday school room in years, and that it really wasn't suitable for a Sunday school room. And, we had three other children's classrooms.

"That's not the point," a parishioner said. "The point is that you thought it was less important to have that space for kids. What do you think that says to the church?" We then jettisoned much of the conversation around the survey to have a deeper discussion about our church priorities, which was quickly forgotten amid the business of our fall activities.

Fortunately, I was able to recognize a few of my mistakes in that meeting. First, I had assumed that everyone in the group would read the survey without emotion. For me, this was a new church where I was just beginning to understand something about the culture, the people, and the programs. In my mind, critiquing a program or practice was different from critiquing the individuals. My parishioners, though, had poured themselves into those small church practices. Every program was because of one or two individuals who poured a lot of energy and emotion into their work.

Second, I had wrongly assumed that, when it came to converting the classroom into a workroom space, that people would understand the justification. We were, after all, maximizing the space for the work that we were doing. Truthfully, most people neither cared nor expressed an opinion. For a handful of people, it was a symbolic gesture. They knew, of course, that I was committed to working with the children and youth. By that point, I was attending youth group every week. Children's programs were a constant point of conversation. For those who cared, though, the symbolism of turning a children's space into a workroom echoed a conversation that had been happening well before my time: Do we need a nursery?

Could the cemetery expand into the playground? More than that, the action tapped into a fear of the congregation, which at the time boasted only a handful of youth and a fourth grader. If there were no kids, could there be a vital congregation? And could the congregation reasonably assume that I would prioritize children if I was so ready to remove the Sunday school classroom?

In a classical economics framework, decisions about programs and classroom space are made by optimizing resources. But most people, as the field of behavioral economics routinely demonstrates, do not make those decisions with such cold calculations. In a small-membership church, such decisions are tied up with a number of factors. Parents remember their kids playing in Sunday school rooms before church. Volunteers recall how fun it was (or how it wasn't fun at all) to work on an event or a program. They remember the feeling of accomplishment for a program, even when it continues long past its natural expiration date. But none of that is bad. In fact, it's all very normal. People hardly ever make cold, rational decisions. Even when they do, as Kahneman points out, they are not aware of it, or they are wrong in their decisions.

This leads to a more pressing question. In the small-membership church, we know the ways people make decisions. If we know that the people in our congregations are going to make decisions in light of their memories, their relationships, and their feelings, then why would we not take account of those things when we create the processes by which we make decisions? Knowing this information, though, means that the leader of the small congregation has built and maintained meaningful relationships. Only then can leaders understand how the decisions are made and help the congregation make decisions that further and support their ministry goals.

My congregation might have made the same decision that I had made, had I structured the decision considering their relationships, feelings, and memories. Later on, after several conversations about how we were intentional about guarding the things most important to our congregation, we became open to using space differently, became more adept at hearing feedback and more open about what values and traditions we wanted to safeguard. In short, had I invested more time in understanding the relationships I would have been able to better communicate our goals and ensure that our institutional memories, hopes, and fears were better addressed in the decision-making process. Had I invested more in understanding the relationships at work in my congregation, I would have been better positioned to address the fears and concerns that arose. I would have been able to lead.

Leading an organization through relationships requires the pastor to pay attention to a few different things. On the one hand, pastors and church leaders need to understand how relational leadership is both similar to and different from other, more hierarchical models of leadership. On the other hand, they need to pay attention to how their leadership is supporting the theological values of the congregation, and how the congregation is being taught to embed those values into their organizational practices. Throughout all of this, leaders of small-membership churches need to understand how relationship-building is an integral part of leading the entire organization.

Leaders in small congregations should account for at least three ways that the social fabric of their congregation will create a framework for decision-making. First, they need to understand the emotional well-being of their congregation and how that will shape their motivations. Second, congregations will need to balance the myriad ways that individuals are interpreting their mission and how those different interpretations are shaping dynamics. Finally, any leader must be aware of the interpersonal politics between members.

ATTENDING TO EMOTIONAL WELL-BEING

Our emotions impact the ways in which we make decisions. In the small-membership church, this is amplified. A mentor of mine once told me that every interaction was an instance of pastoral care. When I became a pastor, those became words I lived by. No, I did not have deep conversations about the well-being of a parishioner's spiritual emotional life in the hallway. Neither did we unpack family systems in budget meetings. This, of course, was not what my mentor had meant.

Rather, my mentor encouraged me to be aware of how people's emotional and psychological lives were shaping the decisions that we made as a congregation. Naturally, that would seep into the way we make decisions and the ways in which we would respond to a situation.

The need to pay attention to the emotions of the room is well documented in management theory. Management scholars Margaret Hopkins and Robert Yonker, for instance, point out that all types of conflict—whether it's a conflict rooted in personal disagreement, a disagreement about which task to perform, or a disagreement about process—are not necessarily rational but will necessarily "incorporate emotional states."[10] Paying attention to, and managing, the emotions of the people in the room with you is important for achieving good outcomes. The tenor of a meeting will change depending on the emotions of the people in the room. If everyone is expecting a tense meeting, the meeting is more likely to be tense. If people start a meeting from a positive emotional place, the meeting is more likely to have a positive outcome.[11]

Small-membership churches occupy a special place in the lives of their parishioners. In churches where multiple generations of the same family were born, raised, and died, the church is a place of constancy. Even in transient communities, small-membership churches are places where people have voice and influence. They are places where they are known, where they feel value, or where they can easily feel discredited. The small-membership church is not just another building in town; it is a core part of our world. As a result, it is not a place where people tend to make cold, rational decisions.

People bring their emotions—their hopes, fears, feelings of loss, their pain, and their joy—into all aspects of life in the small-membership church. While this does not mean that every meeting needs to become a counseling session, the pastor does need to be able to distinguish why a conversation is taking a particular turn.

One Friday morning, I found myself in a breakfast meeting in a small church in Raleigh, North Carolina. I was newly graduated from seminary and serving in what Methodists call "extension ministry," or a ministry outside of the local church. The topic of the discussion was how to get more young people into the congregation. While the breakfast was nice, I found myself frustrated when I arrived at work because I felt like the conversation was fruitless. I was frustrated. As I unpacked the conversation later, I recognized a few different emotional drivers. First, I was tired and stressed. The breakfast was scheduled for 7 a.m. I needed to be at work by 8:15. Since I normally walked, I didn't have a parking pass. Throughout the meeting, I anxiously watched the clock, trying to figure out how much time I would need to drive back to my apartment, park my car, and walk to work. Second, I was annoyed by the focus of the meeting. We had young people in the congregation, I thought. Why can't we just be included in what's already happening? This, I recognized, was less about the meeting and more about my own insecurities, how I desperately wanted my voice to be appreciated and seen as valuable. While I interpreted the point of the meeting as further discrediting that, being invited to the meeting was in fact proof that I was valued. Finally, I noted the sense of care and concern for the future of the church. I wanted to change the topic. The others in the room wanted to put our fears on the table. Our emotions were conflicting, even if we hadn't known it.

In every organization, people bring their emotions into any conversation. When I meet with colleagues to discuss budgets and strategy, those conversations will be shaped by any number of issues: a professor worried about getting tenure, a junior colleague striving for a promotion, an argument with a spouse that someone cannot stop thinking about. All of these concerns flavor our meetings, even when we try to put them aside.

But the gift of the small-membership church is that we bring our whole selves into the congregation. Leaders in the small congregation have the opportunity to get to know and understand the whole being of those under their care. This presents two strengths. First, pastors and leaders can better navigate those moments when decisions go awry. By focusing on the well-being of their parishioners, congregational leaders can better understand when and how to bring up a delicate conversation, or when to move an idea forward. By not separating pastoral care from the pastoral leadership, pastors of small congregations can better navigate decisions.

Second, and more important, because people bring their whole selves into the congregation, we need not rush to put aside our fears, worries, joys, or hopes in the midst of a meeting about budgets. While I'm not suggesting every meeting become a therapeutic session, there will undoubtedly be times when a conversation about facilities, budgets, or even hymns raise sharp emotions. Rather than ignore those for the sake of consensus, the small congregation can work toward healing. Because of the depth of our relationships, any conversation is poised to become a conversation of growth and discipleship.

MANAGING MULTIPLE INTERPRETATIONS

In the first chapter, we looked at the ways in which our theological imaginations are shaped by a myriad of spaces. Our imaginations are shaped by where we work, where we live, our family histories, our culture, and where and with whom we spend our free time. Our imaginations, in turn, shape our vocabularies, and how we understand each other.

On a large scale, we can see this in the ways different geographic regions describe things, even as common as food. Take barbecue for example. In North Carolina, where I spent the first twenty-eight years of my life, barbecue (or properly BBQ) is pulled pork cooked in a regional sauce. In the eastern part of the state, the sauce is vinegar based; in the western part, it's tomato based. When I went to any of the BBQ restaurants in the state, I would walk up to the counter, order BBQ, and everyone would know exactly what I was getting.

In seminary, I visited a friend in Houston, Texas, who took me to their favorite BBQ joint. I walked up to the counter and asked for a

BBQ plate. The man behind the counter stared at me. "OK, but what kind?" He proceeded to list off possible BBQ plates I could have: brisket with a dry rub, brisket with a sauce, smoked brisket, pulled pork, smoked chicken—the list was long and comprehensive. What was a singular, definitive noun in my lexicon was an adjective for a whole type of food.

When I spent a summer in Johannesburg, a friend invited me to his house for a barbecue. What he meant, of course, was grilled food—hot dogs, hamburgers, even some lambchops. Depending on where you are, barbecue functions differently: a specific noun for a specific type of food, an adjective for how food is cooked, or a verb for what you're going to do with the food.

In the small-membership church, people in the room will bring their definitions, shaped by any number of ideas, personal histories, or cultural markers. Basic terms like "community outreach," or "missions" or "evangelism" or even "worship" might have very different meanings in different churches and different groups in a church. Since decisions and conversations are often happening informally, leaders need to be mindful that their vocabulary matches the vocabulary of the people around them.

This gap in vocabulary is not unique to the small church. In my day job, where I manage large, statewide partnerships, one of the most pressing tasks is to ensure that everyone is working off a common definition. Usually, this happens in somewhat formal settings—we issue a memorandum, we agree as a group to define things a certain way, or even write a "project dictionary" that includes what we mean when we say something.

In small-membership churches, communication is less formal. The strength of this is that information can flow rapidly from all corners of the congregation. In the best circumstances, good ideas can flow to the top, no matter who proposed them. But this informality also means that key words can easily be assumed to have the same meaning.

One night, after a long and seemingly unproductive leadership council meeting, two of my parishioners—a married couple—stopped by my office as I was packing up. They were longtime members of the congregation and served in a variety of roles. I had gotten to know them well enough that, even when I tried to disguise it, they could generally tell when I was frustrated about something.

"It seems like you want us to be doing more," the husband said.

He was right. For the better part of a year, we had been talking about doing more community outreach, which we all agreed was a priority for our congregation. I was a bit irritated that, though we had never moved beyond the events that we had always done, there was a feeling of accomplishment in the room whenever we started talking about our work in the community.

The wife listened, nodded, and offered her own observation. "I think everyone here believes we are doing work in the community." She mentioned the craft fair, with vendors from all over the county; the annual father-daughter dance that would raise a few thousand dollars for a local nonprofit; and the two large barbecue dinner fundraisers that would see our church of sixty serve around a thousand people.

"I think the problem," her husband said, "is that no one has defined what we meant by 'community engagement.' Everyone has a different idea about what that means."

It was a moment of clarity. There was a feeling of triumph because, when we reported on our community engagement, there were a number of events that engaged people in the community in meaningful ways. Meanwhile, I was frustrated because I wrongly assumed that everyone understood "community engagement" to be correlated with "missions and service to the community."

While challenging, this can also present a great gift to the small-membership church. Because conversations are informal, it is easier to expand our definitions in nonthreatening ways, allowing the church to capture the local essence of the people in the room and adding to the theological imagination. As I got to know people in my congregation, I recognized that I was actually the one flattening the word "community." My parishioners had a much more robust understanding. We needed a space where people in the area could come and eat with neighbors they might not frequently see. Our BBQ dinners were more than a fundraiser; they provided an essential fellowship space. Community also had familial elements, and our father-daughter dance reinforced that we were a congregation of families.

The relationality of the small church allowed for a fluidity in definitions. While it can be confusing, the depth of the relationships also meant that definitions were constantly expanding. As a pastor, I began to recognize that my job was to help assemble that vocabulary, drawing out the theology that existed underneath them. In essence, the deep relationality of the church made it possible for us to deepen our imaginations, forming our understanding of our own actions and the work of the church.

NAVIGATING INTERNAL POLITICS

Every organization, regardless of size, will have internal politics. To be clear, this is not about the politics of national or state elections, or the political ads that cross our televisions and radios during a tense election. Instead, the politics of an organization is simply the way that decisions are made and enacted. For Aristotle, politics is the means by which a group of people deliberate and act so that the group moves toward the desired goal. Simply put, any time a group of people determines its end goal, makes a decision about the best way to move toward that goal, and then puts that plan into action, politics is happening. Anytime a group of people try to make decisions for the good of an organization, politics will be present. Churches are not immune.

In some instances, these politics might be overt. In congregational churches, where members are elected to leadership teams in open votes, you might find someone actively lobbying people to vote for them. Or, you might find a group of people, frustrated with the prospect of presenting their idea to yet another committee, attempt to bypass a team.

In one small church, the committee tasked with building maintenance wanted to hire someone to paint the hallway. Each time they presented it to the administrative council, though, there was disagreement about whether the church had the finances. Eventually, they came up with a new plan. At the next administrative council meeting, the chair proposed that members of the congregation adopt a room to clean up. The members that adopted a particular room would do a deep clean of the room, and if they saw any issues and felt like donating the funds, they could go ahead and pay for the repairs. The administrative council thought this was a great idea.

A few weeks later, the pastor walked into the building to find a paint crew hard at work in the hallway and the building committee chair sitting in a nearby classroom. "The members of our committee adopted the hallway," he said with a grin. "I noticed the paint was cracked and chipped, so I went ahead and donated the funds to have it painted."

Here, the politics were blatant but fairly innocuous. A committee recognized (albeit through frustration) that their proposal was not gaining traction. They created an alternative, more palatable (though slightly deceptive) proposal, ensuring that they would be able to carry out their goal. Then, they executed the plan.

At other times, the politics are less obvious. A group of church leaders might decide not to carry out a project because they feel like the project would anger a longtime member. A family might refuse to participate in a function, believing that by not doing so they can make a statement or influence future decisions. A lay leader might call the pastor and encourage them to go visit an individual, important to the congregation, who feels isolated from the church.

Like most things, organizational politics are neither always nefarious nor always positive. Rather, the ethics of church politics is how they are utilized. In the small-membership church, where relationships rule, there are times a pastor will necessarily sit in their office and shrewdly calculate who in the congregation will be receptive to an idea and whether or not they can influence others. They will take the member out to lunch or chat with them after the service.

Likewise, there are times when a pastor will drop by an elderly member's house to catch up on the latest goings-on in the congregation because they know they will get honest feedback about how people are responding to new ideas.

Church politics can also be shrewd, though. In a small congregation, individuals are keenly aware when the Staff Parish Relations Committee is stacked with friends of the pastor, ensuring that the pastor never receives honest feedback. This is a political calculation that allows the pastor to alienate swaths of the congregation, shoring up more authority for that pastor. Whether intending to or not, the pastor can circumvent the democratic nature of a small-membership church and create an autocracy, backed by their most ardent supporters.

Likewise, in some small churches, a longtime member, with deep familial connections to the congregation, will invoke their family history to decry every decision with which they disagree. They'll threaten to leave the congregation if they disagree with even the smallest of decisions. This sort of behavior, likewise, can create a toxic environment. The members who threaten to leave are dismissing the opinions of their fellow members, demanding that the congregation bend to their will.

In truth, most congregational politics will happen naturally and without much observation. People will sit over coffee and decide how to deal with an over-the-top personality, gossip will run through a room, and people will advocate for their own ideas and agendas for the congregation. All of these are the natural politics of the congregation at work, and they can be helpful to the work of ordering the church and living out the church's mission.

What makes these politics dangerous, however, is that in a small-membership church, they are deeply personal. More accurately, there is often little distinction between the politics of a church and the personal relationships in a church. Both in my own work as a pastor and in my work consulting other pastors, I often see this play out in interesting ways. As a pastor, I had a disagreement with a person in my congregation who frequently took me to lunch to implore me not to preach about certain topics. After receiving a number of complaints via text and Facebook messages about Scripture selections, hymns, and guest preachers, I suggested she offer her complaints instead to the staff-parish relations committee. She and her husband instead left the church.

In my university work, I am expected to work with people who I may not like and who may not like me. The way that this usually plays out is that we simply interact only when needed—when we sit on the same committee or have a common project. We can choose not to socialize outside of work, and I don't need to stop by their office to chat.

In the small-membership church, though, I am forced to come face-to-face with the people who have hurt me and whom I have likely hurt. The woman in the above example was deeply hurt by my refusal to field her complaints. I was deeply frustrated with the sheer number of complaints. I can appreciate her decision to leave the church, but politics is not limited to one or two people. The interaction we had rippled out. Some members confided that they were pleased that the couple had left. They were not members; they did not actively participate in activities but were quite vocal in their opinions. Other members came to my office begging me to right whatever disagreement might have existed. As you might expect, these discussions rippled out, too. I sat face-to-face with congregants who were deeply hurt that they had lost a friend, holding the knowledge that my actions were at least partially responsible for that hurt. I watched as people discussed all of this among themselves, including the potential rifts over my actions and those of this one individual. It shaped how we made decisions, it influenced administrative council meetings, and even had an impact on giving (in my own defense, net giving went up afterward). It was church politics borne out of a personal disagreement.

It is easy for personal politics to quickly spiral in a small-membership church. But the inverse is also true. Because of the church's relationality, the small-membership church has a resiliency. People who are committed to the institution and each other are able to find ways to move forward even among personal disputes. Major "church politics" can be fixed with a few personal conversations and pastoral care. I was once consulting for a small-membership church in a small town. One parishioner routinely pushed back on the conversation. After a break, the parishioner was much more pleasant, making some valuable contributions. As I was packing up at the end of the session, one of their friends approached me. "I'm sorry about his behavior," the friend said. "During the break, I told him he was being rude, and no one was going to listen if he was being rude."

This was a simple action, but one that salvaged the meeting. More than that, it is one that is uniquely possible in a place where relationships are forged through time and commitment. Such a blunt conversation requires an honesty and trust built through a meaningful friendship. The relationality of the small-membership church is what made our work that day possible.

LIVING TOGETHER WELL

Some of my favorite images from Scripture are those of the early church, found in Acts. The early church emphasized life together, often in small groups, and what we would today describe as house churches. Some of the most important decisions made in the book were about how the community will live well together. In Acts 4, for instance, we see a community sharing resources in order to provide for the needs of each other. In Acts 6, the disciples consider and respond to complaints about the discrepancies in the amount of food individuals were receiving. These decisions about living well together are an important component of the ethics of the church.

The small-membership church is an heir to these communities in Acts. Many of the important decisions in the early church were made because of the deep relationships that existed among the early believers. Building relationships was not one component of pastoral leadership; it was the foundation for pastoral leadership.

In the small-membership church, there is little distinction between the well-being of the individuals of the congregation and the congregation as a whole. When we take this into consideration, we can recognize that leaders of the small-membership church have to pay special attention to the relationships that exist—not just for the sake of getting to know people but so that we can ensure that we are able to have the conversations we need to have, focus on our mission, and deepen our faith together. More than that, our focus on relationality empowers us to move more deeply into discipleship. We focus on the emotional well-being of parishioners because it helps us heal as a congregation. We pay attention to the places where our informal communications can talk past each other because it deepens and expands our theological imagination, broadening our understanding of what our theological task is. We pay attention to the way personal disputes ripple throughout the congregation because, while it might be political, we also recognize that it can be a source of healing.

The relationships of the small church are the foundation for how we *do* ministry. It is the basis for building both the ethics of ministry and the practices of ministry. It is how we learn generosity, gratitude, and hospitality. It is how we come to create systems of confession and repentance. Rather than just being a "quivering mass of availability," this attenuation to pastoral care allows the small-membership church to become a living example of the kingdom of God.

Small-membership churches need not hide from their relationality. It is a feature, not a bug. By recognizing the gifts, we can move ourselves away from the fear of "just being a chaplaincy" to understanding ourselves as a vibrant community of ministry. Our relationality is a gift of the small-membership church.

CHAPTER THREE

The Nimble Small Church

When I work with pastors of small-membership churches, I frequently hear a frustration along the lines of "Our churches don't want to change." On the surface, this might look true. The personal attachments to seemingly innocuous things like where the pulpit is positioned or what happened to the hideous chairs at the front of the church can suddenly turn into huge altercations. In the church where I grew up, the pastor replaced the large pulpit with a smaller podium. He felt dwarfed by the huge piece of furniture. He was surprised by the intense reactions: the adult children who donated the pulpit in their parents' memory, the people who had grown up in the church seeing that pulpit every Sunday and ascribed to it a symbolic authority, and people who just didn't like the aesthetic all suddenly formed a coalition. The pastor put the pulpit back and remarked to me, "I guess change is hard."

Many small churches have important, long-standing traditions that are important and unique to them. Many small churches have long histories that are intertwined with the history of the families within them. When three generations of children have been baptized in the same baptismal font, that font becomes an important icon of God's work in their family. Suddenly disposing of it for a new one for the sake of aesthetic renovations is a likely way to upset someone.

Similarly, in many small-membership churches, people might remain in their leadership roles for years. Or, if committee term limits apply, a handful of leaders might simply rotate committee positions. After a few years as the chair of the administrative council, they move over to become the chair of the finance committee. The policies and procedures that are put into place can become calcified. Because they work well—or at least they did once—leaders are hesitant to change them.

For pastors and leaders entering congregations, this adherence to tradition, the way that seemingly small changes are blown out of proportion, or the ways that committees can function on autopilot can be maddening. Trying to change them can feel like running into a brick wall over and over again. Even when the choice to change a decision can seem inherently rational and logical, the calcified systems stay in place.

In reality, because small-membership churches are deeply relational places, they can be surprisingly nimble, responding to needs and opportunities with alarming speed. Where large organizations will need to navigate complex staff, detailed policies, and layers of committees, a decision in a small-membership church can be handled with a few strategic phone calls and a meeting in the parking lot.

FEELING STUCK

If it's true that small churches are nimble, then why does it often feel like the behaviors of a small-membership church are etched in stone? There are many reasons for this. One fact church leaders need to recognize is that people like the path of least resistance.

In the previous chapters, we looked at the role of behavioral economics in an organization. In the first chapter, we saw that people will respond to the way a choice is structured, a process behavioral economists call *choice architecture*. In the second chapter, we saw that individuals and groups do not always necessarily choose the most rational option, even if they are making thoughtful decisions.

In fact, even when people think deeply about what they do, they do not always arrive at the most rational conclusion.

Let me be clear here in saying that rationality, as I'm using it here, is not a marker of intelligence, thoughtfulness, morality, or intellect. Rather, to be entirely rational is to operate almost as a computer algorithm, arriving at a precise conclusion for any given problem. It is entirely predictable. Each month, I adjust numbers in our family's spreadsheet budget. I know that if I adjust the cost of groceries in one column and adjust the income in another, the spreadsheet will perform the calculations in the exact same way, every single time. It is supremely rational.

Humans, on the other hand, are not that consistent. We can have a consistent moral guide, be deeply analytical, and be supremely thoughtful. We will still be inconsistent in our decision-making and occasionally make choices that are unhelpful to us in the long run. For example, Daniel Kahneman and his team conducted *noise audits* of companies to determine the variability in decision-making. In such an audit, the group would ask insurance underwriters who had the same degree of experience, training, and reputation to assess a premium for the same case. The CEOs of these companies would anticipate that there would be a marginal difference—around 10 percent—between the premiums. Instead, the researchers found that they varied, on average, by 55 percent.[1] Individuals who had the same amount of experience, training, and skill level, who were thinking thoughtfully and rationally about their assignment, arrived at wildly different places. What accounts for the difference? Even when accounting for bias, a variety of *noises* can have an outsized impact on a person's decision-making: Are they hungry? Are they cold? Did they sleep well the night before? Are they in a good mood? Did their pen run out of ink? Even people who are trained to think deeply and rationally will not arrive at entirely rational conclusions.

Part of that decision-making process itself comes down to what decision is easiest to make. As Richard Thaler and Cass Sunstein highlight, the default choice will always be the easiest choice to make.[2] In a church setting, the committee structure that has existed for a long time has become the default. Checking in with a longtime family about a decision becomes a default. And so, even when it becomes irrational to do so, the default structure becomes easiest. Even if the rationality of that is challenged outright, the default may very well win, because even when people are thoughtful, as we have seen, they are not always rational. When churches seem to be static and immovable, it is often because the default decision processes have become well-defined, even if they are leading to not-so-great outcomes.

Another organizational reality church leaders should remember is that changes in a deeply relational organization impact the relationships themselves. I often hear pastors tell stories of times when their attempts at change were foiled. The stories are usually the same. A pastor insists on making a change. Sometimes, it's a change that is deeply insignificant. Other times, it's of great theological importance. A few people become upset with the change. The pastor asserts that their decision is the appropriate one. Feelings are hurt, regardless of whether the change is made. The pastor, venting to friends, will say something like, "This is about what's best for the church. It's not personal. They're going to have to get used to change." It's a predictable story, and it's one that I have told myself.

There are a few issues with such a story. First, the pastor usually makes an assumption about how important or unimportant the proposed change might be. This often serves as a support for the second issue, when the pastor asserts that their change is the only rational and theologically appropriate decision that could be made. As we've seen, even the most well-trained, experienced individuals cannot consistently trust their decisions were entirely rational or unbiased. Third, and most importantly, the pastor assumes that the change is about the larger institution rather than the people within it.

Small-membership churches are built around relationships. The traditions they hold are part of what builds those relationships. Any decision in the church will impact the people who have previously made a decision. Once, I sat in a meeting where we debated about whether to have coleslaw as an option at our annual barbecue fundraiser. What seemed like an inconsequential decision to me was actually a deeply personal one. We opted not to have the coleslaw. I had not realized, though, that the family that typically made the coleslaw had been feeling that, increasingly, their input did not matter. Here, they were offering to produce the same side dish that they did every year, and the church leadership was saying, "We don't really want your contribution." It was yet another in a series of decisions that left them feeling like their contributions were not welcome. Is coleslaw really that important? No. Were they feeling ostracized because, time and again, the traditions they had helped establish were deemed unhelpful? Absolutely.

Another colleague, upon arriving at their church, decided that it was time to purchase new paraments for the altar table. They proposed to throw out the old purple ones and purchase new blue ones. A person in the congregation scorned the decision, deriding the expensive purchase and defending the existing color choice. Sensing a heated conflict, the pastor backed down. A few months later, the parishioner presented a new set of handmade blue paraments. As it turned out, and unbeknownst to the pastor, someone in their family had made the previous set. Their outburst in the meeting was in seeing something that their relative had made be disposed of rather callously. After some thought, they recognized that the paraments had become old and worn. Still, they did not think a handmade set should be replaced with something purchased from a store. So they dutifully handmade a new set in the color the pastor preferred.

Each time that person looked at the altar, they saw a legacy of their family's faithfulness. They saw how their family had given their best gifts to God, and they saw how they were the continuation of that. They, too, dutifully showed up to carry out the church's mission. To throw out that reminder of their family and their family's faithfulness would be callous at best. To replace it with something bought from a store would be to forget about the gifts of the people in the church. It was just paraments, but it was also deeply personal.

Small-church leaders necessarily contend with these realities again and again. The members of the church, including the pastor, will opt to take the path of least resistance, even when they are being thoughtful and deliberate. Following the same decision-making process is the easiest route, even if it leads to decisions that are less than helpful. These decisions are intertwined with the relationships of the people who compose the small-membership church. Deciding to change something often feels personal because it is personal. Damaging relationships over and over to implement change will inevitably harm the church because it will harm the relationships within it.

The good news is that, while these realities make it appear as if small churches are rusted and immovable, in all actuality, they are quite nimble. By understanding why churches appear to be stuck or immobile, leaders of small churches can actually use those very realities to recognize and cultivate the appetite for change that already exists in small congregations.

A SOLAR SYSTEM MODEL

For several years, I had an executive coach. Their job was to help me think through strategic decisions in my work and professional life. For example, I had been constantly frustrated that when I presented a proposal at work, no matter how well researched and thorough, my supervisor would nitpick each detail. If my supervisor asked a question and I had a ready answer, they would grow frustrated, eventually leading to a refrain of, "You can't have all the answers, Allen."

Eventually, no matter how detailed the proposal, my supervisor would find the smallest reason to reject it. In one instance, I was asked to change a list of items from a numbered list to a lettered list. I would make the requisite changes, after which it would be approved. Meanwhile, as a perfectionist, I wanted to demonstrate that I was doing the hard work up front. I worked as hard as possible to ensure that I was anticipating every single question my supervisor would ask. However, the constant nitpicking was making me feel like a failure.

I expressed this frustration to my leadership coach, who responded with a curt, "Why would you do all of that?"

"Because eventually they'll see that I'm working hard, and I'll figure out exactly how to get it approved the first time," I responded.

"That's silly," my leadership coach said. "Has your boss ever approved anyone's proposal the first time?"

"No," I said.

"And he's not going to do it to yours, either," my coach said.

The issue, my coach told me, was that both my boss and I had a problem. His problem was that he would always find something wrong with the first proposal. My problem was that I took that as a disapproval of my work. My coach made a new suggestion, "What would you do if you knew your first proposal would get shot down?"

So, that is what I began assuming. I started scheduling my proposal presentations for earlier in the process, well before I completed all of my research and finished all of my preparation. My supervisor would ask questions that I knew would have to be answered for the final version but did not yet have the answer. Instead of ten-page proposals, I was turning in two-page summaries. A few weeks later, I would come back with a polished, final version. There would be almost no questions, despite the sometimes drastic changes between the versions.

My relationship with my supervisor improved. I got the approvals I needed to do my work. It ended up working well. My leadership coach's advice was fairly simple: You are not going to change this process, so why keep trying? You can actually get what you want by understanding how your audience is acting.

The default decision process was always going to result in a critique of my work. Once my leadership coach helped me to recognize that, I was able to use the default processes to get what I wanted. Rather than attempting to change *how* the decision processes were carried out, I was able to navigate that process to get better results.

When leaders of small churches begin making changes, they often try to change the default decision structures or to minimize the relational nature of the small-membership church. In doing so, it feels like the entire church is resisting change. Instead, churches can use those organizational realities to help create the change they want to see take root and blossom.

John Kotter, a leading organizational theorist, highlights the perks of being a small organization. There is often an assumption that small organizations will have small hierarchies, like a miniature version of a large-scale corporation. Kotter reminds us that this is an erroneous assumption. Small organizations are not hierarchical but are essentially organized networks of people.[3] Successful start-ups, Kotter points out, start out in this relational structure out of necessity.

Rather than a clearly defined pyramid organizational chart with a CEO at the top, a few deputies under them, and a host of project managers at the bottom, Kotter compares these small start-ups to a solar system. The sun at the center is an entrepreneur with a few key others. Extending out from them, in all places, are small initiatives and those who manage them. In this system, even the most junior person (say, the third rock from the sun), can be the most important. Importantly, these planets are not defined areas. Kotter is quick to point out that there is no "marketing planet, finance planet, [or] operations planet." Instead, each planet is an initiative that the organization is trying to test and launch.[4]

Small, successful start-ups operate in this way for some critical reasons. If they are to survive in a turbulent marketplace, they need to be small in order to be agile, fast, and respond to changes in the marketplace. Being in a small network of relationships, these start-ups have better lines of communication and fewer silos. Everyone weighs in on decisions about finance and operations and marketing because every project requires those things. And, since there are no finance departments, someone working on a critically important initiative can simply go ask their colleague working at the next desk for help.

Hierarchies do not actually come into place until later, when organizational structures become an absolute necessity. According to Kotter, these hierarchies eventually overgrow the relational network and can eventually choke it out completely.[5] Large organizations eventually become less agile, needing to navigate complex hierarchies to implement any meaningful change or shift an initiative. This is why Kotter encourages larger organizations to spend time intentionally developing relational networks within their hierarchical systems, so that people can still freely exchange information, observations, and suggestions.[6]

Kotter writes from the perspective of an economic imagination that encourages rapid and sustainable growth. He is writing to an audience of business leaders who are trying to figure out where their successful start-up went stale and how they should respond to market forces. So, what does this have to offer small-membership churches?

It is important to remember that while the church has a different end goal, they still operate as organizations. Even the small-membership church exists within sprawling denominational systems, with layers of bureaucracy and hierarchies. In my own United Methodist denomination, I served as a pastor of a church and reported to a district superintendent, who in turn reported to a bishop, who in turn was held accountable to an episcopal committee. I was instructed to implement a church governance structure that was outlined in our denomination's polity, which resembled all the other churches in our denomination, large or small. The assumption that my denomination makes is that every congregation, again large or small, will have a similar hierarchy and that small churches will just have miniature versions of the large-membership church structures. I recognize that my denomination is not alone in this assumption.

This, of course, is the same assumption that Kotter dispels. The small-membership church, as a small organization, is not built around a pyramid-like hierarchy where the pastor sits at the top and deftly manages committees and work groups. It is much more akin to the solar system model that Kotter describes. The pastor and their vision might be at the center, but they are in a network with all the other groups and leaders within the congregation.

Of course, churches have committees because they are often required to, but in most small churches, decisions are not made in the committee meetings. The committee structure, in many instances, becomes a nuisance as people try to find new members to fill the slots of people, term-limited yet still eager to serve. Instead, I frequently hear pastors complain that the major discussions and debates happen outside of the meeting.

The most notorious culprit is the famed "church parking lot meeting." After church on Sunday morning, a few members will gather in the parking lot to talk about the week's goings-on. By the time the administrative council meeting rolls around that evening, all of the details have been prediscussed. The administrative council will deliberate, maybe even have a formal vote. Then, after the meeting, several members will stop and chat in the parking lot about the meeting they just had. The next day, someone will call the pastor to say, "You know, we all liked the decision we arrived at last night." Or, they'll call and say, "You know, a few of us were talking, and we should rethink that decision."

Most pastors hold a deep disdain for these parking lot meetings, and understandably so. After all, they spend time thinking through the agenda for a meeting, trying to discern the best course of action for a congregation and how it should be implemented. Then, after the decision seems to be made, when the meeting is adjourned, a few members somehow still have the power to change the decision because of a conversation in the parking lot.

Some pastors, naturally, will try to reroute their congregation from those parking lot meetings. They will insist that the appropriate place for discussion and decisions are in the committee rooms when everyone is gathered. And, they will be frustrated when, time after time, the parking lot meeting trumps the actual meeting. As my executive coach chided me, "If you know that's what they're going to do, why fight it?"

These parking lot meetings are a clear example of Kotter's relational network in action. Anyone can be pulled into a parking lot meeting, where the hierarchies of the "official structure" fall apart. The most vocal member of the parking lot meeting might be someone who rarely speaks up in the actual meeting. Or it might be someone who is not officially on the committee but who regularly provides input on the work of the church and whose opinion carries a great deal of weight. The pastor is just another voice, even if they are an important one. Information is freely shared across silos, even if it is not always wanted.

These parking lot meetings are actually a great example of how small-membership churches readily adapt to change. When the relational network presents new information, outside of the typical hierarchical format, the members of that network readily change. They will pivot from a previous position, change key elements of a worship service, redesign entire programs, and revisit previously closed issues. While it can be frustrating to a pastor, especially if the pastor is not involved, it demonstrates how rapidly a small-membership church is willing to change. Granted, at times, the parking lot meeting can result in a status quo decision. But the discussions by the cars also provide valuable information as to why the status quo might be preferred. People reveal their fears, voice their worries, and reaffirm their commitments in these meetings. Far from being a nuisance that reinforces the status quo, these meetings provide a great deal of information about what needs to be addressed before a change can be implemented. It reveals the avenues through which pastoral care can serve as a foundation for future change.

As a pastor, I spent the first year trying to observe the traditions of my congregation and building relationships. As Easter rolled around, I was disappointed to learn that there would be no opportunity for me to preach. The tradition in this particular church was to do an Easter cantata on Easter Sunday, leaving room only for Holy Communion. Sensing a bit of my disappointment, the choir director suggested I add some Holy Week activities. So, we added a Maundy Thursday Service and a Good Friday service.

The next Easter, I chatted with the choir director during a youth group event. I asked if we could have a short Easter sermon. So, as we chatted, we sketched out a plan for a service with the entire cantata and a brief homily. The service was extended from the typical hour to around ninety minutes, and no one complained. By the time we brought it up to the worship committee, it had been well-discussed among members of the choir and congregation. No one batted an eye at the change in service time, and the small sanctuary saw the same large Easter crowd as always.

But I didn't love the service. As we sketched it out, it seemed like a fine idea to move from the cantata to a brief homily. In practice, it was awkward. The choir was tired from their energetic performance. The members of the congregation were engaged with the music and drama of the choir's effort. And then, as it all concluded, the service shifted from something special to church as normal. It made more sense for us to just do the Easter cantata.

So, the third year, as we began planning for Easter, I raised that point. I thought adding in the sermon detracted from the choir's performance—not because it was a bad sermon or badly delivered, just because it shifted the mood and altered the experience.

Again, during a youth group dinner while the teenagers all played basketball, the choir director said, "But you really wanted to do that. You really wanted to preach."

"I know, but I think it might have been a mistake. I don't want to take away from the cantata," I said.

"Ok," he said, "Let's change it back."

There were a few things that amazed me about this experience. First, it defied the expectation that I had about my small church. Not only were they open to change but they offered it at the outset, supporting new worship services. Second, almost all of the decisions took place outside of the worship committee. The bulk of the conversations happened in informal settings, among choir members, at other events, and in more than a few parking lot meetings. By the time we got to the worship committee meeting, we had all but decided what would happen and were just offering a chance to air out any other opinions that people might have.

I also recognize, in retrospect, that part of the openness to the changes was due to not wanting to eliminate what was really important to my parishioners. In an early conversation, I haphazardly mentioned moving the cantata to Palm Sunday, which drew a stony silence. Had I forced the issue, I suspect that it would have made the choir feel unappreciated. Instead, they were quick to support changes, so long as it preserved the traditions that had been shaping the church for decades.

PRACTICES TO STAY NIMBLE

One of the great gifts of a small church is its ability to be nimble and adaptable. That does not mean, however, that these congregations make use of that gift. Like other gifts, the ability to be adaptive and flexible is something that needs to be exercised. In order to make use of that, church leaders should practice four things.

One practice is to acknowledge the places where small-membership churches are already good at change and where they already practice being adaptive and flexible. It might be that volunteers in the worship service are great at filling in when someone has an unexpected absence on Sunday. It might be the way people can quickly pull together a community meal at the last minute. It might be the way people pitch in to help with something at the last minute. These smaller moments of flexibility are often overlooked. By emphasizing them, leaders in small churches can illustrate how flexibility and adaptability are already part of the culture.

Another exercise is to remember that not everything needs to change all the time. Being flexible is great but only if it moves the organization closer to its end goal, its *telos*. In chapter 1, we saw how an organization's narratives, traditions, and practices help a community move toward its ultimate goal, which, for the church, is life in the kingdom of God. There are some practices in the church that beautifully form the community in meaningful ways, where changing them might actually be harmful. There are some changes that neither move the community toward its telos nor detract from it. Why spend energy and social capital on those battles? There are some changes that satiate an individual's personal preference but can really distract from the telos of the church. I once met a theologian, a lay person, who remarked that every time a new pastor at the church arrived, they made slight changes to the worship service. Each time, they would talk about how this was a more appropriate way to lead the service and that their changes were more theologically sound. The result? The laity disengaged from worship planning and viewed that process as something that was rather unimportant. After all, if every pastor changed it, then it couldn't be that important, could it?

Churches should stay focused on their primary telos and build practices that move them toward it. One practical way to do this is to follow Jim Collins's hedgehog concept. Collins proposes creating a Venn diagram with three circles. In one circle, organizations detail the single thing they can be the best at in the world. In the second, they articulate what they are passionate about. In the third, they detail how they find the resources to do that. The place where all three of these circles overlap becomes the goal of that organization. Collins compares this to a hedgehog, whose defense mechanism is to ball up in a way that protects their center, while being able to roll around and avoid threats.[7] By keeping the *telos* at the center of the church life, the church can adapt and be flexible without sacrificing those things that make up its narrative, traditions, and practices. By using this concept, churches can articulate the things that they cannot, or do not want, to change. Those are the three concentric circles: what they are passionate about, what they are best at, and how they secure the resources to do that. Once they have those identified, they can adapt as needed to move closer to their goal.

The third custom leaders of small-membership churches should emphasize is the looseness of their relational networks, rather than attempting to adhere to strict hierarchies and complicated bureaucracies. For pastors in more structured denominational systems, this might be more difficult simply because it is assumed that church structures only vary in the size of their hierarchy and bureaucracy. Kotter reminds us that small organizations, like small-membership churches, are not simple little versions of the same organizational structure. They operate and function in completely different ways.

Embracing the relational networks in a congregation allows decisions to be made in organic ways. Rather than formal meetings, where people may or may not share their opinions, or simply bite their tongue until the meeting in the parking lot, the nature of relational networks allows members of the congregation to freely express their opinions in environments where they are most comfortable.

Decisions and plans get hashed out over coffee, in the hallway, and over dinners. This doesn't mean that the church will entirely dispose of the hierarchies, though. Important work still happens in a meeting. Instead, this embrace of the relational network simply means that church leaders don't view those committees and the church bureaucracy as its primary path to change. Instead, they recognize that most of the change will happen through more informal processes, and finally be affirmed and solidified during the committee meetings.

Embracing this network does require the pastor to do some important work, though. First, the pastor must be able to keep in mind the larger picture of the organization. As people bring new ideas or respond to ideas and proposals from other members, the pastor must help them connect that to the broader mission of the congregation and help them articulate how their work will further that mission. Second, the pastor must act as a connector. As people voice more opinions, the pastor must be able to connect them to other resources, both inside and outside of the congregation. They might call a few members together who have similar interests or compatible skills, or they might connect a member to a neighboring nonprofit. Third, they must act as an interpreter. As people voice ideas and opinions, the pastor must be able to interpret those hopes, concerns, and questions to different members of the congregation.

Acting as an interpreter is especially important to the fourth practice: understanding and appropriately managing the roles of individuals in the organization. In small-membership churches, a single person can be the difference between leading successful change and derailing the work of the congregation. Pastors need to be aware of the influence of individuals in the congregation as they begin leading change, so that they can spend time with the appropriate people, minimize the dangers to their goals, and build broader support for change within the congregation.

In his change management theory, William Bridges notes that when people go through transitions, there are three phases. First, something ends. Later, there will be a new beginning. In between, however, is a neutral zone.[8] Bridges compares this to the Exodus story: Moses leads the Israelites out of Egypt (the ending), they wander through the desert (the neutral zone), and eventually arrive at the promised land (the new beginning).[9]

In each phase, the leader will necessarily contend with a variety of human responses. As people face endings in programs, initiatives, or traditions, they feel loss. Bridges notes that people might begin to disengage from what is happening. If they strongly identified with something, they might find that part of their identity is gone. Or they might simply be disenchanted with the organization. In the neutral zone phase, people are often unsure about where they are headed, or they might feel like things were better before. Some people thrive in the neutral zone, preferring the unknown, while others are afraid of what new thing might emerge. Then, as new beginnings emerge, people contend with what the new beginning means for them, and they contend with their losses in the new reality. If they lost their turf or their identity because something ended, they look for ways to regain those things in their new reality.[10] Using the analogy of the Exodus story, we see this clearly played out: the Israelites leave Egypt and happily rid themselves of their identity as slaves. In the desert, they begin to wonder if they were better off in Egypt. Some are reluctant to enter the Promised Land. When they finally arrive at the Promised Land, there is a change of leadership, as Joshua succeeds Moses, and new roles are established.[11]

Every change and transition, no matter how small or large, will have these three movements and have people experience the kind of loss, disorientation, hope, and worry that Bridges describes. The pastor's role is helped by understanding how individuals in their congregation are responding to these various phases. This does not mean, though, that pastors need to honor every person's emotions or hinge entire decisions and change processes upon one or two people. Instead, they need to be keenly aware of the power dynamics that exist within a congregation.

For example, some members of the congregation will speak loudly and complain often. While they might occasionally have some good input, they are not influential within the congregation. As a new pastor, I had parishioners who frequently invited me out to lunch to complain about happenings in the congregation, send texts and emails with their frustrations, and lecture me about their disappointment in my leadership (on Christmas Eve, no less). When I spoke to my Staff Parish Relations Chair about it, the chair just laughed. "They complain a lot, but they don't have a bite."

Others in a congregation are generally supportive of change. They will be advocates no matter what. They may or may not have influence in the congregation. They might often be pushing the congregation to go faster than they are prepared for, and they almost always have encouraging words to say.

Still others will be more cautious. They will need the change explained to them, they will weigh their personal feelings of loss and excitement against the larger group. They will take seriously the concerns of other members and balance them against the optimism of those who are supporting change.

Finally, some will just be ambivalent, floating wherever the congregation goes. When pressed, they may be supportive or not. This group might be passive participants in the church and are typically not the ones who volunteer to serve as committee chairs. They are present but have no real strong feelings about what happens next.

Pastors need to be diligent in spending their time responding to the right people in the midst of change. Those who are obstinately against any transition, while they might offer good feedback from time to time, will likely never be convinced. There's seldom a good reason to try, unless they hold a large amount of influence or formal power within the congregation. It's better to let them vent and move along. Meanwhile, those who are energetically supportive of change might offer a morale booster, but they also do not need to be managed. Likewise, those who are ambivalent will follow the rest of the congregation.

Instead, effective leaders in small churches spend their time with those who could be swayed. Leaders listen to the fears and take them into account when planning, creating ways to help people feel connected to the broader work of the church. They take those individuals' feedback seriously and incorporate it into the planning process. They spend time one-on-one with the members who are on the fence and help guide them through. They do this because, as a few of these members begin to become supportive, other members follow suit. Eventually, they become supporters who influence others to embrace change as well.

INNOVATION AND SURVIVAL

Author and Episcopal priest Lisa Fischbeck shares a story of her college daughter who texted her with a quote from class: "Evolutionary innovation occurs most easily and quickly in small populations."[12] A small-church pastor, Fischbeck invokes the wisdom of evolutionary biology and writes that, "Small churches can change their meeting time or the way they engage with the surrounding community with surprising swiftness. They can more readily talk about and explain, discuss, and even argue about changes with each other and then break bread together in fellowship." Being small creates opportunities for nimbleness because nimbleness is a trait necessary for small populations to survive.

This is, of course, a trait that we see reflected throughout history. In the eighteenth and nineteenth centuries, American Methodism spread through the nimbleness of small chapels in places most people would not want to be. While other denominations established strongholds in major cities, creating tall steeple churches, Methodism spread as a patchwork of small chapels, many of which consisted of a few families. The result was significant growth—from less than 3 percent of all churchgoers in 1776 to more than 34 percent by 1850. Methodism became the largest denomination in the nation, comprised almost entirely of small-membership chapels.[13]

Or, consider the people of the early church. In Acts, churches are house churches, meeting in the homes of members with a close-knit community. Harley Atkinson and Joel Comiskey note that these churches would likely only have had around fifteen to twenty members. When they outgrew their space, a new congregation would pop up.[14] It was, they argue, this small size that "provided the ideal context for nurture, community, sharing, and evangelism."[15] It was also this small size that protected these early churches from being stamped out in the midst of persecution, since their small size allowed them the ability to pivot and move as needed.

Being small does not mean that the church is incapable of change. In fact, it means that these congregations are better suited for change. Their relational structure allows them to share information and ideas more freely and to execute decisions more rapidly. Small-membership churches do this regularly, providing pastoral care at a moment's notice to a grieving family, altering calendars to accommodate for someone's schedule, or organizing events at the last second to take advantage of a good opportunity.

That relational structure also means that churches cannot default to existing as a small hierarchy. Rather than attempting to force change through formal structures, pastors and lay leaders must manage change through the networks of relationships. This connectivity, after all, is the evolutionary gift of being small. It is the same gift that allowed the Christian faith to spread throughout the world. Being small does not mean that change is impossible. It just means that it has to be managed well. More importantly, it means that churches can quickly embrace change that will bring them closer to their vocation and similarly reject the changes that will not. The relationality of the small membership will bristle against changes that cause fear because people do not want to lose what is central to their identity. At the same time, they are able to rapidly embrace that which deepens their discipleship. This experience can only happen if we lead through the relationships of our congregations.

PART TWO

The People of the Small Church

CHAPTER FOUR

Choosing Small

The easiest rebuttal to everything we've discussed so far is simple: So what? Sure, small-membership churches may be relational communities that can quickly adapt in ways that make them deeply formational. But who is attending small-membership churches? Part two of this book explores that question. Who shows up to small-membership churches? And why are these churches a preferred place for the people who attend? In this chapter, we'll explore what it means to choose small, diving into some of the data about the people who choose to attend these congregations. In chapter 5, I will explore the myth of the aging small congregation.

WHAT IS SMALL?

As the National Congregations Study makes clear, while most churches are small, most people attend larger churches.[1] In that report, they note that 91 percent of churches house roughly half of all churchgoers. The remaining 9 percent of congregations house the other half of churchgoers. So, while the average congregation size is around 70, the average churchgoer worships at a church of 360.[2]

At first glance, this statistic can be read to assume that small churches are doomed. If nearly half of churchgoers attend the largest

9 percent of churches, then is there a future for the small-membership church? To lapse into economic language, is there even a market for small churches?

Well, yes. We know that because the same data tells us that about 50 percent of all churchgoers choose *not* to attend the largest churches in the United States. To be fair, not all of those congregations are considered small. So, are people attending small-membership churches?

The truth is, the definition of a small-membership church can be a tad controversial. A pastor in South Dakota, Zach Kingery, pointed out to me that *small* is a relative term. Kingery is a United Methodist pastor in the Dakotas Annual Conference, which consists of both North and South Dakota. Of the United Methodist Churches in that Annual Conference, only three of the 231 congregations are above that 360 average worship attendance mark. Another nineteen congregations have an average worship attendance of a hundred or more, which means that the remaining 209 worship with ninety-nine or fewer people each week. Within that context, the average worship attendance of the largest twenty congregations is around 235.[3] Kingery prefers to not talk about "small" vs. "large" churches. Instead, noting the lower average worship attendance in his context, he uses the language of "normative sized."

Or consider the Texas Annual Conference, which includes a portion of the state and is headquartered in Houston. There, the average worship attendance for the largest twenty churches is 1,081. Kingery's point is valid and well taken. Small in Texas is quite large in the Dakotas.

For the sake of this chapter, though, I want to look at churches with fewer than one hundred people in average worship attendance. I recognize that some denominations in some places will scoff at the idea of ninety-nine people being small. Meanwhile, in other areas, they will wonder why I did not set the measurement higher. I chose this number for two reasons. First, to borrow Kingery's language, the normative church size in the United States is around seventy people.[4] Second, churches below a hundred tend to have similarities in how they behave and how they are organized. Third, and most selfishly, the data in the National Congregations Study is segmented in ways that make it easier to analyze.

Armed with an adequate definition, we can better answer the question about small-church attendance in the United States. Using the data available in the National Congregations Study, we can look at how attendance has changed at small and large churches. In 1998, in the first study, roughly 14.6 percent of churchgoers attended a church of fewer than a hundred participants. Meanwhile, 44.9 percent attended a church of five hundred or more. In the 2018–2019 study, the percentage of people attending churches with fewer than a hundred people had grown to 20 percent, while the share of churchgoers attending churches of five hundred or more dropped slightly, from nearly 45 percent to 43.5 percent. Meanwhile, the share of people attending churches of between 250 and 499 dropped from around 19 percent to around 16 percent.[5]

I am not suggesting that large churches are in decline—the numbers don't support that at all. In fact, the percentage of people attending churches with more than five thousand people rose a bit. Nevertheless, it is worth noting that the share of people attending churches of fewer than a hundred people continues to rise, while some mid-size and larger congregations, on average, declined in the share of people participating in their congregation.

These numbers reveal that a decent percentage of people are choosing to remain in small-membership churches. We also know that these people are engaged in their congregations. For instance, the National Congregations Study noted that people in larger congregations give less. A church of a hundred receives an average of around $2,000 per person, while a church of a thousand receives an average of $1,350 per person.[6] And, as we will explore in chapter 6, members of small congregations are committed to the life and work of their churches.

So, what does all of this mean? Primarily, it means that there are people who not only wind up in a small-membership church; they are intentional about belonging to a small-membership church. They are committed to the community they find within that congregation and find it to be a compelling expression of faithfulness.

A SENSE OF BELONGING

When I was in college, I began attending the Wesley Foundation, a United Methodist Campus ministry. At the time, I wasn't part of the United Methodist Church, and I really wasn't all that interested in the religious aspects of the group. I went primarily for two reasons: they let me play my guitar in worship, and a lot of my friends from orientation were going.

The Wesley Foundation had four banners that hung around our meeting space, reflecting our core values: Ask, Grow, Serve, Belong. Over my four years, I asked a fair number of questions, found a place to grow in my faith, and went on a few service trips. Those were all important to me. But none of them were why I stayed in the group, or even why I became one of the student leaders.

If I'm completely honest, I stayed in the group because of that fourth value: Belong. As a freshman, walking onto a new university campus where I didn't know anyone, this campus ministry gave a me a sense of belonging. I knew that, if I showed up on Thursday nights, I would find a free meal, play my guitar in worship, and see my friends. Even if my closest friends weren't there, I would have someone with whom I could sit and eat, crack jokes, and hang out. My comfort in asking questions, spiritual growth, and community service all grew out of that sense of belonging.

People have an innate desire to belong to something. Over the last several years, even prior to the COVID-19 pandemic, researchers noted that loneliness was becoming a "major public health and policy concern."[7] These researchers subsequently found that, as had been widely reported, loneliness increased during the pandemic, as social and physical distancing precautions were put into place.[8] The precautions put in place to keep us healthy also required a significant adjustment to our lives. As a result, we found ourselves searching for a connection to others.

Church life requires a sense of belonging, of connectedness. Church life requires community. That connectedness happens more naturally in smaller groups of people, where relationships are built and nurtured. Larger institutions have, of course, known this for quite some time. Large-membership churches have long recognized that small groups are an essential element to growing their congregation. Priscilla Pope-Levison points out that megachurches often rely on small groups to attract new participants.[9] In these instances, small groups are a way of inviting people to participate in a comfortable, non-intimidating environment.[10]

Fresh Expressions is a church revitalization movement that also depends upon forming meaningful connections that help people belong. Citing the statistic that more than 60 percent of people do not attend church, Fresh Expressions seeks to help find alternative ways of helping people engage in their discipleship. According to the Fresh Expressions website, a fresh expression initiative revolves around asking "How can I help my friends connect with God?"[11] A fresh expression might be a group meeting over dinner for conversation about contemporary events through a theological and scriptural lens, or it might be fishing together. Other Fresh Expressions take place in pubs and breweries, while a few happen in yoga studios. At the core of all of these, though, is finding a common interest that connects others and building community around it.

In both Fresh Expressions and large churches with dedicated small groups, there is a clear understanding and articulation about the necessity of belonging to something. Simply showing up at a worship service with seven hundred or five thousand people is fine. That event, though, is not where the hardest work of formation, of connecting to God and connecting to one another, will happen. No, that work will happen in the small groups and the relational ministries of the congregation, where people can find a way to belong. In short, these movements replicate the most important element of the small congregation.

Obviously, there are some core differences between these small groups and the small congregation. The small groups in a megachurch and the intentional outreach of a Fresh Expressions gathering differ significantly from that of a small-membership church. The groups in the former are intentionally designed to connect new

THE GIFT OF SMALL

people, to be points of entry. The multiple small groups are built to be replicated, facilitating engagement among more people.[12]

The small-membership church might be a point of entry into congregational life. More likely, it is a place of formation for those who are part of what Carl Dudley calls, "the fabric of the group."[13] This caring cell, as Dudley calls it, supports members and is deeply intimate but can also be hard to join. It is designed to nurture and support the members that are already in it, and joining it can be a difficult process. This can be a strength, as people are committed to the life of the congregation, can be vulnerable with one another, and can build a deeply formational community. It can also manifest in unhelpful ways—treating newcomers as intruders or not making space for people who are searching for a place to belong.[14]

THE CHOICE OF SMALL

The National Congregations Survey describes the average attendance of churches like this:

> To get a feel for just how concentrated people are in the largest congregations, imagine that we have lined up all congregations in the United States from the smallest to the largest. Imagine that you are walking along this line, starting on the end with the smallest congregations. When you get to a congregation with 360 people, you would have walked past about half of all church goers, but more than 90% (91%, to be exact) of all congregations.[15]

I have heard this statement interpreted in a few different ways. Some tend to quote it as proof that the majority of our churches are failing. They are small, and therefore they are not sustainable. To get to our most vital churches (and here, vitality is falsely equated to growth), we have to walk by the majority of all of our congregations. How is it, this argument goes, that only 9 percent of our congregations are really growing?

But there is another way to view this, one that I think is much healthier. Half of all churchgoers are intentionally choosing to be in their smaller congregations. Almost one in five chooses to remain in a small-membership church with fewer than a hundred people. They've chosen to be there because it is a place where they can belong.

When I was the pastor of a small-membership church, I felt constant pressure to compete with the churches that were booming around me. There were tall steeple congregations, new church plants, and megachurches with multiple campuses. Their worship services were slick productions, well-choreographed. Ours were messy. A fuse blew in the electric organ, and the sound guy was on his hands and knees during my sermon, trying to replace it. A youth would walk into the service and walk down the center aisle to sit with his family, squashing the final, emotional part of my sermon that I worked so hard to craft. An elderly woman would request to play a song on the piano that was really special to her with no notice.

All of that was fine. It was our own messy community. We knew the man crawling around to fix the organ really wanted what was best for the church. The youth was a stalwart, always ready to help out. The church was really this woman's only social outing for the week. We wanted to care for them, to help them grow in their faith, to nurture them, and to be nurtured by them.

I often bristled at that messiness. How would we ever compete with the congregation that had a truly great worship band, a world-class professional choir, or a state-of-the-art pipe organ? But then, I would talk to the people who chose our congregation. There were plenty of them.

There were young adults, not much older than me, who had ventured out of the larger nearby churches to find something that they described as, "simpler, more authentic, more personal." There were recent retirees who wanted a closer community. There were teenagers who came just because their friends came.

Of course, some people left for other churches, too. They wanted something bigger. It's a story that many pastors of small-membership churches share. Lewis Parks highlights the logic of those moves, writing that the people who move to those congregations want more access to programs. But Parks also knows that small congregations have their purpose. He writes about those families leaving his congregation. "What I did try to do is figure out what the alternative logic might be for a small church. And I think it might be this: the small church offers a surrogate family for those whose basic family unit is dispersed or in need of wider circles of reinforcement."[16]

By focusing on becoming bigger, small-membership churches can actually sacrifice the essence of who they are. That there are so many small-membership churches is not a testament to their failure to thrive. Rather, it's a testament to the fact that people enjoy participating in these congregations. If every small congregation grew into a large congregation, where would these people who crave those wider circles of reinforcement end up?

This reinforcement is not just about social realities, either. It is a theological reinforcement to remind us of our deepest values. One Sunday, I showed up to preach at a small congregation. Before the service, the lay leader told me he would lead the prayer requests. During that part of the service, he stood between the two rows of pews and gave instructions. "We'll start here and work our way around." He nodded at the first woman. "You have anything you want us to pray for?"

One by one, we made our way around the sanctuary, where the lay leader dutifully asked each member if they had any prayer requests to share. And they did. They shared deeply personal challenges. They shared hopeful news about recoveries from illness. They talked about their grandkids' teachers. They asked for guidance. Then, after we had made our way around the sanctuary, and every person had shared, the lay leader nodded at me, ready for me to carry all of these heartfelt prayer requests to God.

If I were visiting that church, I would be deeply uncomfortable. Would I be willing to share something personal? Probably not at first blush. But after a few Sundays, after a few lunches and coffees, I would start to trust these people who prayed for one another every week. And I would know that prayer mattered. I would know how to pray, and I would know how to be in community.

On the drive home, I remembered a moment from my undergraduate days. My roommate at the time was an atheist. He wasn't anti-religion. His family wasn't religious, and one time, he shared with me that he had never really considered religion. One night, he decided to tag along for our weekly Wesley Foundation service. We ate dinner, I helped lead the musical worship, and our campus pastor gave the message. At the end, we formed a circle, and we shared prayer requests for each other. Finally, one of the students who close us out in a group prayer. Afterward, a smaller group of the student leadership team would go pray for each of the prayer requests individually. Each member would commit to praying for an individual's prayer request throughout the week.

When we got back to the dorm, I asked my roommate what he thought about the whole experience.

"What was that part at the end?" he asked me.

"What do you mean?"

"Where everyone just shared things."

I explained that it was where we asked other people to pray for us.

"I was just surprised because people shared really personal things. With strangers."

But really, we weren't strangers. We were a small group of people who had found a place to belong. This is what I find in small congregations.

THE PARADOX OF CHOOSING SIZE

People often encounter a paradox as they choose small-membership churches. On one hand, the small-membership church for many people is a place that they consciously want to be. They choose to remain in a small-membership church because the intimacy of the congregation is formative to their theological imagination and their habits of discipleship. The community of the small-membership church is a testament to the community of the kingdom of God.

On the other hand, by inviting others into that community, they risk altering what makes their congregation significant. At some point, if the congregation continues to add new participants, it outgrows the sense of being a small-membership church. By getting larger, members of the congregation risk giving up the aspect of their identity they have become best at.

Often, the people who choose small congregations find themselves seemingly caught between these two starkly different realities. Their congregation is a place of deep theological and personal formation, but they also can be told that if they're not attracting new members, they're failing. To do the latter would mean fundamentally altering the former.

Small churches approach this paradox in different ways. Some churches are adamant about getting bigger. There's nothing wrong with that. For these congregations, there is a recognition that growing larger will change the fabric of the congregation. For each new person added, the church will need to readjust its understanding of its identity as a caring cell. Eventually, that single-celled organism will necessarily need to split into multiple groups. The intimacy of the church will necessarily morph into intimacy that takes place in multiple spaces, among multiple groups. For some churches and some congregations, this change is not a bad thing, particularly if they feel a calling to be a larger community, to a different organizational vocation, to practice discipleship in different ways. We should celebrate that.

At the same time, many small-membership churches will embrace their vocation as being a small congregation. They are a small group unto themselves, committed to each other. Sociologically, their congregation has arrived at a point they, consciously or not, feel is the right size for their vocation.[17] Growing too rapidly will alter that. Because evangelism is a necessary part of any congregation's mission and vocation, they will need to determine how exactly they bring new people into relationship with God and with each other.

There is a way to thread this needle. For some, that might be through avenues like Fresh Expressions. For others, it might be seeding a new church down the road, a new partner congregation where people who need it can find a similar caring cell. For others, it might mean stretching the fabric of the congregation and discovering that the few new individuals add to the fabric.

For many smaller congregations—if not most of them—there is another reality. In an age where church participation is declining across the board, the majority of small congregations are not destined for dramatic size increases. Churches in areas where populations may or may not be increasing, or places where the population is relatively stable, may themselves only remain stable. In these places, the evangelistic mission becomes one of keeping the fabric of the church intact. New members of the community replenish the congregation. As members of the congregation leave, new members take their spots in the fabric of the congregation.

The long-term stability of a congregation is not proof that it's ineffectual. The congregation that consistently renews its social fabric as members move away, die, or leave for other reasons, is actually demonstrating an effective evangelism. Their stability is indicative of reaching new people and inviting them to participate in the community. The pattern of their social fabric changes over time, as people bring in new personalities, but ultimately, it is the same fabric, perpetually repaired and replenished.

The small-membership church that is perpetually replenished is indicative of a healthy institutional vocation. Here, the church is practicing evangelism, acting as a formational body, and encouraging discipleship. This church knows who it is called to be and is actively embracing the traditions, practices, and the narrative that helps it along its journey of discipleship. By shifting from a mindset dominated by the need to grow and embracing those attributes that make it a formational community, the church actually lives into its vocation of being a vital expression of the kingdom of God.

THE SMALL CHURCH IN ACTION

When my oldest daughter was about six months old, she caught the respiratory virus RSV. On a Friday, she spiked a fever of 102 and had a bad cough. We took her to the doctor, who said to monitor her breathing, give her Tylenol to reduce the fever, and keep an eye on her. If her breathing got worse over the weekend, we would need to take her to the ER.

On Sunday, she went to church with me, where a young adult in nursing school kept her in my office, keeping a steady eye on her while she napped. After church, her breathing was more labored. We could see her rib cage each time she took a breath, and we decided to take her to the hospital where she was promptly admitted and put on oxygen.

It was December 17. The next few days were a blur for me. The nurses monitored the flow of oxygen, trying to wean her off. Sets of grandparents rotated in and out of the room. My wife and I made an uncomfortable bed on the floor beside her crib, stacking blankets together to try and get sleep. We took turns going home to shower, then rushing back to the hospital with more food and supplies.

My daughter was released from the hospital on Thursday, December 21. That Sunday, Christmas Eve, I would need to lead two services at my congregation. Typically, bulletins were due by Wednesday, so the chair of the worship committee could print them off. On Wednesday morning, the volunteer emailed with a mostly completed bulletin for each service. She gave me an update of all that had happened while I was out. They had to cancel an event but didn't want to bother me. They worked out some stuff with the choir and recruited some Scripture readers to help fill in the gaps in the services. They made sure that there was a pretty good song selection. We finally finished planning the services on Friday.

I don't remember much from those services. What I remember most is that throughout the process, my parishioners demonstrated that things could run without me. That they cared about my family and would only bother me with work stuff when absolutely necessary.

They texted me all the time, called me to check on me, and asked if I needed anything.

It wasn't compassion reserved for the pastor at one of the busiest times of the year. It was compassion that they demonstrated to everyone. It also wasn't compassion absent theology. They wrote liturgy, kept up our discipleship programs, and planned services. Their commitment to our community became a reflection of our faith. And it was an attractive one, welcoming new members into our social fabric, allowing them to contribute to our community in their own ways. They weren't perfect. I can remember a few non-welcoming moments, a few tough conversations, and a few things I wish we had done differently (even without reflecting on all of the things I wish I had done differently). Still, they were sincere in their desire to be more faithful. Their smallness helped them to do that.

I want to be careful not to romanticize small churches, particularly when it comes to how people choose small. Still, there is a reason that people choose the small church. The small church is a place that helps people uncover their own vocation, helps them understand what it means to be in a Christian community, and helps them articulate their faith in new and tangible ways. It is a place where they belong: to a community, to a faith, to the story of what God is doing around them. People choose small churches because they are a shining example of the kind of commitment the gospel demands. For that reason, these churches need not abandon their vocation as small. They should embrace it.

CHAPTER FIVE

Small, Aging Congregations

There are some pieces of common wisdom that we circulate in the church world. Typically, this advice points out red flags that churches should avoid or leadership maxims that we hold as truth. One of the most timeless examples of such advice is that churches absolutely, without any doubt, should spend a great deal of energy recruiting young families, youth, and young adults. We're told that the church that fails to become younger is doomed to die. There is an assumption that small churches are particularly vulnerable to aging. The remedy, then, is to attract newer, younger members.

If we're going to better understand and appreciate the gifts of the small-membership church, we should explore the validity of these assumptions. First, is it true that small-membership churches are primarily older congregations? Second, if it is true, does that mean that church sustainability and viability require attracting more young people? And third, are there any benefits to an aging congregation?

There is one quick note worth mentioning here. For much of this chapter, I use age sixty as a measuring point. I do that primarily because the National Congregations Study uses that as a cutoff point. There are some flaws with this notion, in a society with longer life expectancy and where people are working in their careers longer. Moreover, as we will see in the final portion of this chapter, it does not adequately capture the disparate stages of life of being a "senior citizen."

FACTS AND FICTION

First, let's address an uncomfortable truth. The average age of people who participate in religion is getting older. According to the National Congregations Study, in the most recent survey from 2018–2019, 43 percent of adults were over sixty years old, a significant increase from 1998, when 29 percent of adults were above the age of sixty. Similarly, the 2018–2019 survey reported that 24 percent of adults were younger than thirty-five. In 1998, that demographic represented 30 percent of church participants. So, there is no arguing that church participants, across the board, are getting older.[1]

Smaller churches are no exception to that. According to data from the National Congregation's Survey, the number of churches with a majority of people above the age of sixty increased across the board, except for churches above five thousand people. Smaller churches actually saw a smaller, though still substantial, increase in the number of churches with a majority above the age of sixty. Even still, our churches are aging, because the people who attend church services are aging. That is not relegated to just small-membership churches.

There is a consistent myth that small-membership churches are composed off mostly older adults. In this narrative, small churches are full of retirees so there's little hope of the church surviving into the future. Fortunately, there is ample data to help us examine these myths. Fair warning: there are a lot of numbers in the next few paragraphs.

Like other congregations, it is true that small-membership churches are aging. Look at two different small-church sizes: churches that average fewer than fifty in average worship attendance and churches with between 50–99 in average worship attendance. In 1998, roughly 19 percent of churches with less than fifty worshippers reported that 56 percent or more of their participants were above the age of sixty. In the 2018–2019 study, that rose to 41 percent. For churches with between 50–99 worshippers, that same number rose from 13 percent to 23 percent. Over the last twenty years, these congregations have gotten older.

This does not mean that these churches are made up entirely of senior citizens or young people. These numbers tell us the opposite, in fact. In churches averaging fewer than fifty participants each week, the distribution between churches with a congregation consisting of a majority of adults over 60 was around 42 percent, while another 40.5 percent reported that that demographic made up 44 percent or less of their congregation (meanwhile, nearly 17 percent of those congregations said that the above-sixty crowd accounted for between 45–55 percent of their congregation). Only 10.6 percent of the churches said this demographic accounted for 90 percent or more of their congregation.

Or, consider the churches averaging between 50–99 people in worship. Nearly 52 percent of these congregations reported that adults above sixty made up 44 percent or less of their congregation. Only 23 percent of the congregations reported that the same demographic accounted for 56 percent or more. Only 3.1 percent of these churches reported that this demographic accounted for 90 percent or more of the congregation.[2]

This data highlights two significant points. First, there is no denying that churches are aging. But they are aging in churches of every size. Second, while more small-membership churches had a majority of participants over the age of sixty, it wasn't the majority of these congregations. The stereotype of small-membership churches that are made up of mostly senior citizens is one that is easily put to rest by a quick glance at the available data.

WAYS THAT AGE MATTERS

There is another question that must be answered here. Why are we so obsessed with having a younger congregation? Is that really the key to vitality?

At first glance, the logic of having younger churches seems to be airtight. As older members die or move away, someone needs to be in the community to take their spaces. Young families will raise their kids in the church. In turn, those kids will eventually, even if they move away, have families in a church. Moreover, having a few young adults will attract other young adults, because, as we've seen in chapter one, the fastest-growing churches tend to be homogeneous. Younger families beget younger families, and in turn, beget stable churches.

In much of the church vitality literature, this has become the only viable path to a thriving church. So much so that I often hear even pastors of large, growing churches lament that their newest members have reached or are close to reaching retirement age. To be vital, conventional wisdom tells us, is to have a young church.

For many churches, particularly in growing suburban areas that attract young families, this may be the case. Similarly, if a new church is starting in a quickly growing part of a city where young adults seem to be congregating, it would be silly not to focus on young families as the church-start launches. Both of these leadership decisions are highly contextual ones.

Yet, there are a myriad of reasons why a congregation might not focus on lowering the average age of the congregation. First is the reality, again, that churches of every size are aging. Second, we might borrow a page from economic developers and argue that aging populations can be a good thing.

We often imagine that suburban communities are replete with young children, minivans, and soccer teams. But many suburban communities are designed to appeal exclusively to recent retirees. These active retirement communities sell a lifestyle that appeals to recent retirees. Early developers of these communities, such as the Del Webb communities or The Villages in Florida, chose to place these communities in suburban places, where amenities, such as access to continuing care facilities, health-care facilities, and access to entertainment was readily available. Suburban places provided an additional boon because land was cheaper than urban cores, and there was no need to be located within commuting distance to a strong job market.[3] Even Jimmy Buffett has cashed in on these elderly enclaves, launching Margaritaville-themed retirement communities for those "aged 55 and better." When the community opened for down payments in November of 2017, more than 150 prospective buyers camped out in the parking lot.[4]

Rural communities, likewise, are increasingly attractive to recent retirees. Because rural communities have lower costs of living, rural communities are often enticing to retirees seeking a slower pace of life while allowing their funds to go further. Noting that more than 1 in 5 adults over 65 live in rural communities, rural communities are investing in new entrepreneurship programs for recent retirees. Because senior citizens move to the community with years of career experience, they can consult existing businesses, mentor new business owners, or even start new businesses in their new rural homes.[5]

All of these initiatives recognize a few positive attributes about the generation of recent retirees. Not all of these will be true for every senior citizen. One positive attribute is that retirees who are relocating to assisted living communities, or who are being tapped for rural entrepreneurship and community development initiatives, often have higher disposable incomes and less debt. While recruiting young families is nice, young families tend to have less income because they have not yet reached their peak earning potential. Additionally, young adults tend to carry high levels of debt—student loans, car payments, and early mortgages or high rent. In the rural community where I previously lived, the tuition at our local daycare facility for one child is roughly $500 a month. In my current city, affordable daycare starts at around $800 a month. In other communities, the cost of daycare can double that. Young adults are prized for being the lifeblood of the church, but they are ill-positioned to make significant financial contributions to a community. The same is true of congregations. Young adults, just starting their careers, lack the financial resources to give significant funds to donate to their congregation.

This is not to say that every recent retiree or senior citizen in a congregation is economically secure and wealthy. Indeed, a substantial portion of our senior citizens are economically insecure, working part-time jobs after retirement, straddled with medical debt, limited opportunities for retirement savings, or even caring for a parent, child, or grandchild. My grandmother, for instance, lived a meager life after the unexpected death of her husband, forcing her to put three kids through college on a secretary's salary. She lived frugally, saving coins to afford bus tours with the local senior citizens group. There is no reality in which she would have the financial resources to open a new business.

Another good thing about recent retirees is that they tend to have more volunteer hours to spend. Theologian Kathleen Cahalan points out that, for many, this period of life is an opportunity to explore talents and skills that they might not have had previous time to explore. During early adulthood and through the middle-aged years, time is spent maintaining a household, shepherding a career, and a myriad of other things. Senior citizens with no kids at home have a freedom to explore and create. Even the Peace Corps has begun recruiting people fifty and up.[6]

While young adults with kids are often cherished within the church, with ample programs to support them, the amount of free time available for additional volunteer activities is significantly lessened. As the parent of two young kids, I can safely say that there is precious little time for any additional things. Volunteering at events or attending meetings at night has to be carefully orchestrated around time with our family, the occasional work trip, babysitter availability, and prior commitments. Meetings during the day are generally out of the question.

While retirees might have some commitments, like working a side job for social interaction, or picking up grandkids after school, there is also ample time to explore interests and passions. Church organizations, as Cahalan notes, have generally recognized this, with agencies like the United Methodist Church's NOMAD ministry, where retirees with RVs travel around the country volunteering. Or, the Encore organization's Purpose Prize, which celebrates individuals over sixty who work for the social good.[7]

This leads to the third asset, which is that senior citizens, generally speaking, have a great deal of experience. Senior citizens bring with them a vast knowledge base acquired through their professional careers, volunteer activities, and lived experiences. My congregation once held a health fair where retired nurses reviewed prescriptions and offered blood pressure screenings. They did not give out medical advice but did encourage people to consult with their doctors if they noticed anything unusual. In a few cases, this was advice that resulted in primary care providers changing medications for members of the congregation.

Even in less formal programs, the knowledge and skills gained over a lifetime can be used in meaningful ways. Retired accountants can provide help solving the inevitable financial problem. A strategic leader can be a sounding board to the pastor, to help think about the mission and vision of the church. Teachers can help students in the church gain literacy skills, or just be a presence for kids and teenagers.

None of this is to say that young adults or middle-aged adults don't have skills or that senior citizens should have a monopoly on such roles in a congregation. Neither is it to say that the experiences, advice, and skills of senior citizens are automatically superior to those of younger generations. Rather, there seems to be a natural tension that exists in churches that are aging, which again, is most of them. On the one hand, we often want to, and rightfully so, include younger voices in our congregation. I've worked and served in places where there were no opportunities for people of my generation, and where people in their final years of retirement would hear no advice or feedback from anyone who had less than twenty-five years of experience. I can vividly recall sitting in a meeting where a young colleague offered a compelling and well-researched suggestion. The most senior leaders roundly laughed at it, based on outdated assumptions. This is not healthy in any organization, much less the church.

At same time, the pendulum can swing too far in the other direction where the voices, skills, and experiences of senior citizens are roundly diminished. This is often what I hear in the consistent drive to make our churches younger—that churches with large numbers of older adults are dying churches. Notice, though, that while there are plenty of criticisms about the nature and purpose of active-living retirement communities (like The Villages in Florida), that business model is not one that seems to be dying out. While there may be a time when such a model pivots, it is not today. Similarly, while churches need to prepare for a day when their communities are changing or anticipate demographic changes around them, it is damaging for the congregation to assume that a large number of people above fifty make the congregation a failure.

VOCATION IN THE AGING CHURCH

Rather than lament that older adults make up a significant portion of our small congregations, we should explore the ways in which small congregations are uniquely situated to leverage these gifts. The small-membership church has a twofold opportunity to cultivate vocation. First, the church is able to cultivate vocation for the senior citizens within the congregation. In turn, those senior citizens help other age groups, particularly young adults, on their vocational journey.

Vocation in late adulthood can take many shapes. Part of that journey, Cahalan tells us, is in "shedding the false self" that has been built up over the years. Cahalan writes that

> There may be parts of people's lives they are not proud of, actions taken that bring shame and guilt, or stories they hope remain hidden. Late adulthood is a pivotal time to grapple with a truer self because people may have the emotional energy and strength to engage the hard work of forgiveness, and in some cases, reconciliation with others, capacities which may become diminished in older age.[8]

As people settle down into retirement, they have an opportunity to make sense of their lives and to think about what comes next. The small church becomes an ideal place to do that, as the entire life of the small-membership church requires living into a community. The deep relationships at the core of these congregations means that individuals must approach the church with some degree of honesty about themselves. In a healthy, close-knit community of friends who love you and people you respect, you learn truths about yourself that you have long wanted to deny, appreciate the nuances that others have always appreciated, and forgive yourself as others forgive you.

But this vocation is not entirely a journey of self-discovery. It is, as Cahalan reminds us, primarily an integrative journey. Citing Richard Rohr, Cahalan reminds readers that as recent retirees begin to understand their identities, they must also learn not to reject that identity. Rather, one of the central questions is how to honor who they have become while creating new space for what is to come in the second half of life.[9] The church, in this place, can become an incubator, a place to try out new interests. Some of that can be internal to the church. An accountant who has always dreamed about public speaking can learn to be a liturgist or a lay speaker, for instance. A chemist can volunteer as the choir director.

That work can also be shared downward, to younger generations. As leaders in economic development have already discovered, older generations have much wisdom to share. Small-membership churches can also be a place where mentorship is cultivated as a formational practice. Importantly, this type of mentorship need not be formal.

Mentorship often naturally develops on its own, like in a workplace. Over the years, I've found that I have collected relationships with people whom I respect, who I turn to for advice and feedback: a professor that I call to ask questions, an experienced pastor to help me think through issues, a local business leader to talk through strategy. Most often, this happens with people who are senior to me, and often with people who are retired or close to retirement.

What I appreciate about these relationships is that, over time, they become mutual. I learn something from my mentors, and in turn, they invite my feedback as I grow. In these relationships' best moments, there is a humility that exists between us. I am not trying to "prove myself" or impress them, and they are not trying to be all-knowing deities. We share a vulnerability, which invites mutual questions. I am able to share my shortcomings and ask for the help and guidance I need; they are able to share what they've learned, often by sharing their mistakes and regrets. In doing so, we come to a deeper understanding of our whole selves.

The small-membership church, where relationships are indispensable, is an important place to develop such relationships, and not simply for the social benefit of the mentor and mentees. More importantly, such a relationship becomes a spiritual practice, reflecting an imagination of the world where the community is nurturing and affirming, building vocations for everyone. As Karl Barth has argued, work rightly understood and rightly ordered happens in the context of a community that helps people understand their gifts and use them in a way that offers glory back to the Creator.[10]

This type of mentorship serves both generations. The older generation begins to do the integrative work that Cahalan correctly deems as necessary. Additionally, they use their skills, wisdom, and knowledge to help shape the future generations. Rather than dispensing of their talents, they are put to meaningful use. Meanwhile, the younger generation is helping their elders in that integrative work—asking honest questions, borne out of vulnerability and demanding vulnerability, seeking out guidance both from what went right and what went poorly. They are also adding to their own skillsets and experiences, acquiring knowledge and wisdom that helps them gain vocational clarity and imagine scenarios that they never imagined.

All of this fosters a new imagination of what it means to have a vocation. When my oldest daughter was born, an older mentor told me, "Your vocation is about to change, because you are a parent now." Rather than seeking out every opportunity for career growth, I began asking questions like "What is a good quality of life? What will be best for my kids?" My mentors helped me make sense of my world. And, as a mentor once shared with me, my questions help them reflect on their lives.

By focusing on developing vocations among those in their second half of life, small-membership churches actually invest in the well-being of their youth and young adults. Rather than isolating generations from one another, generations are joined into a mutual relationship that reflects the social framework of the kingdom of

God: a common table where everyone's gifts are cultivated and used for God's work in the world.

The opposite can also be true. By focusing on one generation at the expense of another, (for instance, overfocusing on young adults and teenagers at the expense of senior citizens) a small-membership church can actually damage relationships between generations and damage our imagination of vocation.

A few years ago, my wife and I were leading a youth Sunday service in our local church. I preached on the story of David and Goliath, noting that David's faithfulness, borne out of what could perhaps be a youthful naivete, led to Goliath's defeat. After the service, an elderly woman approached my wife and me to voice a dissatisfaction. She told us that she felt like the constant attention on youth and young adults was the church saying to her, "Hey, give us your money, but sit down, be quiet, and wait to die."

The tactfulness of the comment can be debated, but it does reveal a tension that exists in several corners of society, including within the church. The constant focus on increasing youth and young adults in the congregation left this person feeling like her voice didn't matter, that she was not capable of contributing anything meaningful to ministry. That in turn gave rise to a competitive streak, a desire to prove that they still had value.

In the workplace, we see this all the time. As people work longer, and find their value and vocation in their work, and as new employees come into the workplace, a natural competition emerges. On the end are people close to retirement, with experience, valuable skillsets, and deep knowledge bases. At the same time, they have certain procedures and ways of doing things that can make them resistant to new ideas. On the other end are young and ambitious people who want to learn, who have new ideas to test out. Yet they often don't have the experience needed to implement those ideas, lacking the ability to see nuanced challenges in front of them.

Here, we might find an opportunity to exercise the type of mentorship described above, where out of humility, the differing generations are able to mutually support each other. But, as Barth reminds us, the nature of sin is to distort what should be. In a broken world such as ours, work becomes primarily about the individual, which can confuse legitimate needs for shallow desires. As a result, a destructive competitiveness emerges that ultimately limits anyone from understanding their full potential.[11]

For instance, many of my colleagues and peers in institutions and churches can remember a senior leader who, rather than taking an opportunity to teach complex skills by having younger professionals join a team, would purposefully exclude them, citing their lack of experience. Or, as one peer noted, too many mentorships are borne out of insecurity. The mentor wants to prove their effectiveness, cement a legacy, and pass on their wisdom. But as their mentee grows, the insecurity manifests. Rather than practice a mutually vulnerable mentorship, they become competitive with their mentee. Because the mentorship was never rooted in the desire to affirm or to help, it becomes toxic to everyone involved.

The small-membership church, by nature of its relationships, can be a place that offers a meaningful alternative. It becomes a place for those in their second half of life to develop a new vocation, to practice new skills, and to make sense of their entire self. In doing so, they also help those who come behind them. They are able to share their triumphs, but sometimes more importantly, their defeats. As a result, the entire community is made stronger.

THE OLDEST ADULTS

There are multiple generations among what we call senior citizens. Not every senior citizen is in great health, nor is every senior citizen active in the community. We might make a distinction between senior citizens in these still active years and senior citizens who are in their last years of life. The latter group is living in what Joyce Ann Mercer refers to as older adulthood.

Intentionally, I wanted to illustrate that *senior citizen* is not synonymous with decline because, as I often notice, when people make blanket statements about aging small-membership churches, they are not conjuring images of active senior citizens. Rather, given the constant narrative of the small-membership church as a chaplaincy, these congregations are portrayed as being filled with senior citizens who are living out the last days of their lives, with few people behind them to take their place.

My grandma was an active member of our small-membership church. When I was a kid, she sang in the choir, served on committees, and volunteered at just about every church function that happened. By helping out in the church, she became part of something bigger than she was. At some point, though, she became too frail to really help out. Her singing voice deteriorated with age, and sometime when I was in high school she could no longer sing in the choir. She developed a tremor that prevented her from being able to help out in the kitchen at church, and eventually, after a few surgeries and an accidental leg break due to brittle bones, she really could only show up on Sunday mornings.

For most of my life, after church on Sunday, we would eat lunch at my grandma's house after church. Often, I would stay after lunch and spend the afternoon with grandma. As I got older, we would spend those afternoons just talking. We would look through photographs, and she would tell me stories, or we would talk about church, about faith, and life.

Stepping down from choir was a monumental event for her. Even if it wasn't acknowledged by the congregation as a whole, her closest friends knew it. About that time, I was becoming more active in the music ministries of my small church, playing instruments to accompany the choir. One year, I was playing bass in the small ensemble, accompanying the choir's annual Christmas cantata. (When I say ensemble, I mean me, a pianist, an organist, and a trumpet player who the choir director knew.)

After rehearsal, several of my grandma's friends streamed over to me. "It's our first cantata without Jean being in the choir. We really miss her." After the cantata ended, we were all invited over to the organist's home for a small Christmas party. I'm not sure why I went, as an eighteen-year-old surrounded by adults two, three, and four times my age, but I did.

The hostess, Sara, made a short toast, thanking all the members of the choir for their contributions to the life of the church and for giving her a group of friends. She looked over at me, and said, "And Allen, we all miss your grandmother. I saw her sitting with your parents tonight, and I know she's proud of you. But we sure do miss her in the choir every week."

Stepping down from the choir was a loss for my grandma's identity, and she grappled with how she was supposed to serve her congregation, and by extension, her faith. This was the question she posed to me one Sunday afternoon, asking, "Is there any way for me to still serve?"

I gave her a short answer. "I guess you can still pray for the church?"

"I guess, but I want to do more."

There will be some who quibble with the framing that prayer is not doing enough, and I am not arguing that prayer is insufficient. But such an argument risks detracting from a real pain at the center of what my grandma was trying to express. As Mercer points out, "most descriptions of vocation have a forward-pressing, positive tone associated with growth, while [our] descriptions of aging speak of decline, debility, and even suffering."[12] My grandma was facing this shift from forward facing to rear facing. There would be few new opportunities to discover, limited time for new talents to emerge. She was growing frailer, and her accomplishments would mostly belong to the past.

Mercer suggests that the vocation for these oldest adults is twofold. First, their vocation is a demonstration of appreciating the act of aging and dying. In doing so, they detach us from ideals of beauty and cultural aesthetics, and instead remind us of the beauty of our created selves. Helping these oldest adults embrace that is a central part of our work as a congregation.[13] Second, their vocation is to uncover an urgency to life, a reminder that things happen now, and lead those around them to embrace life a bit more.[14]

This is important work because it teaches younger generations how to complete a life of faith. When a child is born, we covenant to raise them in the faith. In those years before death, we illustrate how to die well. That happens naturally in a small-membership church. As a high school student, that memory of the Christmas party stands out to me because it was indicative that my grandma's life was well-lived. She was loved, and remembered, not because she was the greatest singer in the world but because people knew that she loved the congregation. Their insistence of that to me made me proud of her, and it made me want to be like her.

In most small-membership churches, one cannot easily hide from aging and dying. The church has a responsibility to care for these members, to help them die well by reorienting their vocation toward that which Mercer describes. In turn, that vocation teaches younger members something about what it means not only to die well but also to live a life of meaning. This happens naturally in a small congregation where kids and our oldest adults sit side by side every week.

Small churches need not fear the myth of the aging congregation in decline. Instead, they ought to embrace the vocational realities that accompany them and celebrate the opportunity for deep spiritual and theological formation.

PART THREE

The Work of the Small Church

CHAPTER SIX

Fewer Programs, Focused Leaders

In this third part, we turn to the work of the small-membership church. Given the theological and organizational attributes of the small-membership church and the motivations and work by people who choose to be part of these congregations, what does the work of these congregations entail? This section will explore this work in three ways. In this chapter, we'll again look at the theological and organizational realities of the small-membership church and begin reframing what meaningful work looks like in the church. How does the work of the small-membership church build upon the natural strengths of its congregation? In chapter 7, we'll look at the important work of developing vocations and ways that the small-membership church can help parishioners understand their vocation through a theological, economic, and sociological lens.

Before all of that, it is important to clarify a few definitions. First, the phrase "work of the church" is a tad ambiguous and loaded. In many circles, the work of the church is purely theological, taking place in the formational settings of worship, teaching, and spiritual formation. In other settings, the work of the church is about the church's activities and programs: small groups, potluck dinners, kids' programs, and outreach ministries. Ideally, these activities are aligned with the theological mission and vision of the church.

In this section, I primarily look at the latter through a theological and organizational lens. After all, when people dismiss small churches for being inactive or sleepy, they are often saying that nothing much happens outside of Sunday morning. The criticism is aimed at small-membership churches not because of their worship or spiritual life but because of the lack of organized activities outside of worship.

Ideally, church activities should be theological and formational. They should help the congregation on their journey of discipleship. So, while I am mostly discussing the activities of the small-membership church, I want to ensure that it is viewed through a theological lens. The theology of the church, after all, should shape the activities of the church rather than just be peripheral to it.

MORE PROGRAMS, MORE VITALITY?

In the first chapter, we explored how our economic imagination shapes the way we think about success in the church. Because we often conceive of success as being equal to more—more money, more profits, more services, more production—we tend to carry that idea of success to the work of the church. So, a successful church, a good church, is one where a lot is happening all the time. I often hear churches, for instance, talk about themselves as a seven-day-a-week church where every day there is a church-led program or group meeting. In the United Methodist Church, our denominational indicators of vitality reflect this. A denomination-wide study demonstrated that more programs and small groups indicated more vitality.[1]

The idea that churches need to be doing something makes sense. After all, almost every organization is measured by its activities and impact. A business must offer a good or a service. Churches, likewise, have scriptural mandates for service to the community and to provide opportunities for spiritual formation.

Small-membership churches without a plethora of activities throughout the week also come under criticism for not making the most use of their space. In rural places, it is not uncommon to drive by small congregations that sit empty and unused throughout the week. As one church leader lamented, there is property worth literally billions of dollars sitting unused throughout the week. In urban and suburban spaces, small churches might represent valuable property. One pastor from a small, urban congregation, pointed out the enigma of having a small congregation worship weekly on what was quickly becoming sought-after real estate. What did it mean that his congregation came week after week to worship and work in this space that was being handed over to developers? Would his church be more valuable if it relocated and the property sold? How do we measure that value? Would it be better for the church to remain but with more programs and activities? Or are there other options?

All of these questions, ultimately, are ones of value. Can a small congregation make an argument for its value in our society if it is running limited programs—or any programs and activities at all? What value are they contributing to the wider community?

These questions emerge from the imagination about economic success that we previously discussed. The ultimate goal of the church—which is meant to be theological—becomes one of programmatic offerings. The question by which churches become graded is not, "How well are you forming the people in your congregation?" but rather, "How many programs are you creating that drive numerical growth in participation?"

Rather than attempting to answer that second question, small-membership churches should again look at the particular strengths that they offer. In better understanding the particularities of their congregations, they can focus on forming people through the ways in which they already participate in the church. By overfocusing on numerical growth, small-membership churches can lose sight of the natural gifts they have to deepen the spiritual lives and theological imagination of the people in their care. When small-membership churches focus on numerical growth, they risk burnout and exhaustion, simply because their organization may not be prepared to support the programmatic efforts needed for numerical growth.

To be clear, I am not suggesting that small-membership churches should abstain from offering intentional programs that are formational in nature, nor that they should avoid being missional entities. Small-membership churches are well-equipped to offer deep spiritual formation and be an active witness to the hope of the gospel within their communities. In order to do that well and meaningfully, however, small-membership churches must do so in ways that draw upon the natural elements of their congregations.

THE ROLE OF LAY LEADERS

Like all ordained clergy in my denomination, I went through a mandatory continuing education following graduation from seminary. The three-year process had regular retreats where we would learn from more experienced clergy about church leadership. Frequently, I would hear that the biggest challenge facing our congregations was apathetic laity. One pastor described laity as if they were on a cruise ship, taking advantage of programs and offerings, rather than wanting to go "be the hands and feet of Jesus."

My lay leader attended the session with me, and on the two-hour drive home, we talked extensively about apathetic laity. There was a deep disconnect between my lay leader and that pastor's perspective, and rightly so. Sure, there were some people in our small congregation who did very little in the church, but we had a high proportion of active members. They served on committees, took on special assignments, organized events, came to Bible study, and helped with worship. Whenever we had a major church event, most people in our congregation would turn out to help.

The biggest challenge, I noted, was one of expectations. At times, I felt like the church wanted me to provide more programs. But when it was time to launch those programs, people were tired, exhausted from the myriad other tasks they were already doing in the congregation. I wondered if that was the disconnect between the speaker and my lay leader.

Such a disconnect is grounded in data. As the *National Congregation Study* highlights, larger churches tend to have higher numbers of people whose participation is limited to attendance at a worship service. Small-membership churches, with smaller staffs, require their leaders to be more engaged in the leadership of the congregation. Relatedly, small congregations, though they have smaller budgets, tend to receive more per capita than their larger church peers—meaning a higher percentage of the congregation gives, even if the overall budget is less.[2] While they have fewer people, small-membership churches also have higher rates of participation outside of worship. These data points reflect the strengths of large and small congregations. Large churches have more people engaging; small churches have fewer people but a higher rate of participation. Large churches have larger budgets, while small congregations have more consistency.

But this raises an important question. If small-membership churches have a higher percentage of volunteers, why would they not be capable of doing more programs and activities for church members and the wider community? To answer that question, it's important to look at the ways that people engage in their congregation. Research on volunteering in nonprofits can shed some additional light.

Broadly speaking, there are two categories of volunteers: regular and episodic. Regular volunteers are typically engaged in an organization over a long period of time. Therefore, they tend to be placed into high-skills volunteer roles. Episodic volunteers, on the other hand, generally show up for one-off events, plugging in where needed.[3] Both types of volunteers are habitual, though the length of time between their volunteering activities might vary. The regular volunteers might volunteer with the same organization every Saturday, for instance, while the episodic volunteer shows up for the monthly or quarterly event.[4] The two types of volunteers rarely engage in the same types of activities, as researchers found that they largely engage in "completely separated circuits of programs."[5]

Importantly, both types of volunteers are motivated by values. In fact, episodic volunteers tended to see themselves as more driven by their values, "stressing religious and civic sense of duty."[6]

In small-membership churches, as Chaves et al. note, there are fewer staff members overall. While large churches have higher number of staff members per capita, researchers speculate that this is possible because of their economy of scale.[7] This allows staff members to take up operational work while handing off non-sensitive assignments to episodic volunteers. For example, in college, I worked in a large congregation. Whenever we had an event, our facilities crew would come and help set up and break down the event. A luncheon, for instance, was supported by a part-time cook, a facilities person, and a clergy person who would plan out the content. Vacation Bible School was coordinated by a staff member who would have volunteers helping manage the actual event.

In that environment, volunteers were essential, but they were episodic. Volunteers might come to the luncheon, but staff handled logistics. For Vacation Bible School, volunteers shepherded kids from site to site and even taught some of the modules. But staff purchased materials, ensured the rooms were set up adequately, and that all the complex logistics like room reservations and budgets would be handled.

Conversely, with only one staff member in a small-membership church, any event was a major undertaking, usually with volunteers filling the most substantial roles. For a Wednesday night meal, a team of volunteers would plan the menu, buy the food, prep all the materials, and cook it, spreading their work out over the course of a few days. Another team of volunteers would set up tables and chairs. Everyone would help clean up. If there was a worship service after, we would leave our mess in the fellowship hall, rush over and play our parts in the service as choir members, liturgists, and myself as the pastor. When the service was over, we would head back to the fellowship hall to break down tables, take out the trash, and wash dishes. At Vacation Bible School, volunteers would chair the planning team, create registration processes, teachers would be responsible for setting up their rooms, volunteers would purchase and cook food, and a team of people decorated the sanctuary. In those events, I took directions from the volunteers.

When thinking about the type of work to be done, small-membership churches need to consider the ways that their volunteers engage in their congregations. The way in which people engage through their volunteer work creates default structures. As we've previously seen, within behavioral economics, default structures are the structured ways that subtly influence choices. In small congregations, the church size itself creates a default choice for volunteering. Because of the limited staff, volunteers are needed for the church operations. Volunteers are the finance chairs, the treasurer, the worship coordinator, and the facilities director. Groups of people take turns cutting the grass and cleaning the sanctuary.

Of course, there will be some volunteers in larger churches who are regular, and there will be a handful of volunteers in the small-membership churches who are episodic. But by and large, the ones who engage in the life of small-membership churches are engaging in operational, behind the scenes tasks. The key volunteers in the small-membership church are not just coming to one or two events a quarter. They are serving in multiple roles that keep the church functioning.

There are a few challenges that emerge. First, regular volunteers, like the ones in our small-membership churches, will need to stay connected to the broader mission of the church. As researchers discovered, episodic volunteers tend to have more idealism about their work, perceiving a deeper impact.[8] Because it is less frequent (even if it is still habitual), their volunteering feels less mundane, less rote. As researchers put it, the episodic work retains a "novelty" about it.[9] This presents a challenge for volunteers at small-membership churches who perceive that their work is becoming staid and boring or that they are not making a significant contribution.

This dynamic does not mean, though, that these regular volunteers are not motivated. Instead, these volunteers show up because they have built relationships with the community of volunteers.[10] The reward for showing up, day after day, week after week, is the deep community that is built in the organization itself. This type of connection can be a powerful asset.

The second major challenge is one of overcommitment. The creation of new programs or initiatives will inevitably require laity support to manage it. After all, small congregations do not have the deep staff support to manage a plethora of initiatives and programs. It is no secret that pastors often feel overburdened in small-membership churches.[11] There is less attention on burnout among laity in small congregations. As a pastor, I remember being chagrined when a parishioner expressed how tired they were by the constant meetings. When I moved into a role at a university and began attending church, I found myself in the same position. On Wednesday nights, I would leave work, pick up my child from daycare, and bolt over to the church, where we had a congregational meal and my wife and I led youth group. Other nights of the week, I would venture down to the church for hours-long meetings, hungry from no dinner, annoyed that I didn't get to say goodnight to my daughter, and tired from a long day of work. I found myself bristling whenever a pastor suggested that laity weren't doing enough. By asking congregants to both manage the operations and tasks of the congregation and insisting that they manage new initiatives that are better suited to episodic volunteers, church leaders risk creating a culture of burnout within their congregants. Our laity in congregations are already working full-time jobs, parenting children, taking care of their aging parents, and volunteering in other parts of the community. Demanding that they take on additional roles that are not aligned with why they participate in the congregation in the first place risks burnout. Rather than just launching new initiatives, the church needs to consider the risks of losing our laity from overwork.

THE WORK OF FORMATION

Ultimately, engagement with the church is about spiritual and theological formation. By suggesting that small-membership churches refrain from needlessly launching new initiatives that burn out their laity, I am not suggesting that these churches do nothing. Rather, I am suggesting that small-membership churches take on the difficult work of formation using the existing structures of the congregation. If the default choice for small congregations is to engage in supporting the work of the congregation, then small-church leaders should leverage that to create formational opportunities in the work that laity are already doing.

There are a few natural ways to do that. As we have seen, the relational nature of the small-membership church is of the utmost importance. Regular, recurring volunteers show up because they are committed to the community of volunteers. They have built a network of friends, and they come back, time after time, to participate in that community.

To put it into more churchy language, volunteers at small-membership churches help at events not because they're convinced that any program or mission will change the community but because they have found a place where they belong. They find a community where their skills are valued and utilized, where they have friends and companions, and they return to that work because the people around them matter to them.

This difference between the motivations of episodic volunteers and regular volunteers is significant for the ways in which small congregations offer formational opportunities. For larger churches, with episodic volunteers, the constant question is how to get those habitual and infrequent volunteers to participate more regularly in the life of the congregation. For instance, imagine a family of four—the parents and two kids—that shows up each quarter for a church's quarterly mission day. On that Saturday, the family of four shows up, receives their job assignments, and dutifully goes to work. They pick up trash, or paint a porch, or any number of activities. Outside of the weekly worship service, their only real engagement in the congregation is in that quarterly event. They don't participate in Bible studies, don't show up for youth group, and aren't active in any committees.

For the staff of the large-membership church, the most likely path forward would be to leverage those mission days in a way that gets them into some sort of small group. Maybe the church begins putting together a pod of families who work on the same assignments every month to build relationships. Maybe they start a Bible study targeted to the people who show up at the mission days. Ultimately, their goal is to move a family from habitual, but infrequent, participation into more regular and formational engagement. In doing so, they connect the work of the church to the theological and spiritual development of the church.

For these congregations, laity are frequently working at the church. In a church with an average worship attendance of sixty, laity are singing in the choir (with a volunteer choir director), are helping prepare the church each week for worship, and showing up to finance committee meetings. For the larger church, the goal is to help members get plugged into the life of the congregation in a more regular way, to help them build relationships so that they want to participate in small groups and leadership work. For the small-membership church, the goal is very different. The small congregation's goal is to help members bridge the connection between their ongoing work in the church and their spiritual formation.

CHAPTER SEVEN

Developing Vocations

Because of the type of relationality at the core of small-membership churches, and because so many people are involved in the operational work of the church, there is a distinctive opportunity to cultivate vocations. By shaping an understanding of vocation, the small-membership church offers an alternative to the imagination that pushes for largesse. More than that, a grounded, theological understanding of vocation helps anchor people in their work in the broader community, whether they are acting as parents, working in an office, teaching school, or wherever else their careers and interests take them. For the Christian, understanding vocation is ultimately about understanding our role within the kingdom of God. The small-membership church is well positioned to help many members explore and name their vocational realities, providing support and encouragement as they understand and live out their vocations.

DEFINING VOCATION

In high school, we were required to take a class on vocational skills. I chose computer skills because it meant that for most of the day, I could quickly do the assignments and then chat with my friends. But I was told these skills were essential to the vocation I would have. Later, in seminary, I was asked to articulate my vocation over and over again.

Like many of the words we use, our context shapes our under-standing of the word *vocation*. Prior to the Reformation, vocation was intrinsically tied to religious, social, and economic station. As historian Sandra Beardsall points out, pursuing vocation as a clergy person was a way to improve one's station in life.[1]

During the Reformation, Luther connected our day-to-day work with our theological understanding of vocation. Later, John Calvin reinforced the idea that both the work and station of a person was that in which they were born. In essence, Calvin and Luther bound vocation to a moral vision of work.[2] Calvin and Luther's idea that vocation is formed by one's station at birth would give way to the notion that all work is theologically and morally good. Work and vocation became tied together.[3]

While the Reformation was arguably effective at dismantling the clerical political hierarchies, Reformers reinforced social hierarchies. This allowed for a divorce between theological reflection and notions of work. Ideas of labor, work, and vocation were connected, but those were separated from spiritual, moral, and theological considerations.[4]

The unintended and unfortunate outcome of Luther and Calvin's teachings on vocation is that they split the theological from the secu-lar. In turn, vocation could be formed in any number of spaces, the church being one among many. But while the term "vocation" might be used in the classroom, in the marketplace, or the social sector, it lacks a common telos. The telos of a soldier's vocation is going to be substantially different from the telos of a teacher's vocation. Neither of those has the same telos as that of a businessperson.

In everyday conversation, it can become simple to use "vocation" and "career" interchangeably. And our work might have a deep call-ing underneath it. My sister, a nurse, has always felt called to the work of a nurse and is exceptional because of it. But we should resist the idea that all work is vocational and that all work is morally good. A businessperson who regularly cheats and swindles their clients might feel called to a wealthy lifestyle, but it would be dangerous to assume that because they work hard, their work is moral.

In a world without sin, in which all of creation is properly ordered, it would be appropriate to say that all work is good because all work would be ordered toward our divine telos. But, as we discussed in chapter 5, our understanding of work and competition is disordered because of sin. Theologian Karl Barth rightfully argues that in a properly ordered world, all work would provide for the needs of both the individual and the community. This work would be formed through "the development of our particular abilities and corresponding accomplishments."[5] The discovery and nurturing of ability would affirm our created selves and offer glory back to the Creator.

However, the world is disordered because of sin. Barth reminds us that the realities of sin make this ideal impossible for three reasons. First, modern work is overly individualized, rending the community and damaging our theological understanding of the self. In turn, work is not geared toward the fulfillment of needs and the affirmation of gifts within the community, because work is no longer coordinated among the whole community. Finally, the individual is no longer able to ascertain their own needs—their "daily bread"—but instead confuse their needs for shallow wants.[6] Work in this disordered world, then, becomes rooted in pure competition, thereby diminishing the opportunity for a person to realize their full created potential. This competition perpetuates the brokenness of the world.[7]

Obviously, competition is an integral part of our economic system. Yet, even Adam Smith, the father of free-market economics, recognizes that competition within the economic system must be used in a way that offers justice for the broader society rather than simply advocating for the best interest of the individual.[8] Smith did not proffer competition purely for the sake of competition, remarking that when an individual "views himself in the light in which he is conscious that others will view him, he sees that to them he is but one of the multitude in no respect better than any other in it."[9] This societal view requires the individual to "humble the arrogance of his self-love, and bring it down to something which other men can go along with."[10] For Smith, competitiveness can only be useful insofar as it expands opportunities for societal flourishing.

Some theological practitioners have attempted to renegotiate the language of vocation in an effort to account for this disordered reality. Steven Garber, for instance, presents a slightly healthier approach, insisting that vocation is about caring "not only for our own flourishing, but for the flourishing of the world."[11] The strength of this argument is that it embraces the complexity of our world and the myriad places where people are formed. Garber spends significant time examining the disordered realities of culture, positing vocation as a means by which we respond to and participate in the healing of that disorder. Garber insists that Christians are "implicated" to act, and through our vocations, we "find a way into that vision" of the kingdom of God.[12]

The fault in Garber's argument lies not in its conclusion but rather in the practices by which he arrives there. Garber correctly insists that flourishing can be cultivated through ordinary and normal practices by ordinary people.[13] However, Garber's examples are not ordinary people filling ordinary positions, but rather through an inverted idea of exceptional people doing ordinary work. Garber highlights eleven examples of his companions as "ordinary people." Of these, ten of the examples graduated from elite schools, like the University of Virginia, Georgetown, and Wake Forest University. The remaining individual was an employee of the World Bank, which hardly constitutes an "ordinary workplace."[14]

In Garber's writing, what makes his companions' vocation compelling is that these graduates of highly selective institutions chose career paths that are atypical of a graduate from those institutions. Rather than demonstrate that vocation can happen in unordinary places, Garber seems to stress that vocation requires the ability—deserved or not—to engage in elite institutions but be willing to choose an alternative path. In doing so, Garber inadvertently falls into a trap of making vocation into a privilege.

Katherine Turpin criticizes the approach to construing vocation in this way. Turpin notes that even in our current society, college education is not necessarily the norm for the "typical young adult."[15] Any conversation about vocation must necessarily reflect the nuance and diversity of experiences across socioeconomic ranges. Even when considering only the experiences of young adults, vocation must be able to account for the differences between young adults who float between jobs in the gig economy and young adults who decide to go straight into the workforce after high school.

Notions of vocation that make sense only within the context of career choice and college education only deepen the disordered economy that Barth illustrates. As Cahalan correctly notes, "If vocation does not make sense in relationship to persons in a variety of social and cultural contexts, it does not have much to contribute to our communities today."[16] Any understanding of vocation must be accessible for all members of a community and congregation, not just those who are able to pursue jobs, educational opportunities, and passions. It must also account for the individual who feels stuck in a dead-end job, the one who never had the opportunity to attend college, the teenage parent, and the elderly member whose opportunities for new careers are behind them.

Rather than reduce our understanding of vocation to being synonymous with careers and work, we should think about vocation as having at least three essential components. First, vocation should be oriented toward the flourishing of both the individual and the whole community. Barth is correct that our understanding of anthropology is damaged by a disordered notion of community. This disordered community leads to unhealthy competition, rather than coordination. While Garber's insistence on vocation as flourishing is correct, that flourishing must invite everyone in the community to participate. It cannot simply be deeded to a privileged few, as Cahalan and Turpin helpfully remind us.

Second, if vocation is related to flourishing communities, then our understanding of what it means to "flourish" must be defined in light of our Christian faith. Here, Long's theological analysis of economics is helpful. While people are formed in a variety of spaces, Long insists that one of those narratives must ultimately be persuasive.[17] Those narratives are closely related to the virtues we cultivate. So, within the church, our virtues "assume a particular narrative, the narrative of God's revelation in Jesus."[18] Our understanding of flourishing reflects the virtues of "faith, charity, and hope."[19] Long ultimately argues that this reflects a notion of what he calls "divine economy." In such an economy, "we present our gifts to God, and in doing so, we are not alienated from them, but we and they are taken up into God's own life."[20] Because our flourishing is connected to our virtues, and our virtues are centered in the narrative of Jesus's work in the world, we understand flourishing to be part of the larger economy of God. Understanding vocation as flourishing helps us to understand our work as revealing the imago Dei—the image of God—within the individual and the community.

Finally, because cultivating vocation is about helping both the community and individual flourish, and because that flourishing is understood through the story and work of Christ, cultivating virtue is ultimately a task of orienting and reorienting the whole community toward the divine. In order to ensure that the gifts and labor of individuals contribute to the whole of the community rather than deepen competitive divisions, vocation becomes linked to the formation of virtue, which happens within the context of a community pursuing their telos. This is what makes vocation compelling. It is extraordinary because it offers a different pattern of life, helping people to understand themselves in light of something bigger than the world.

Vocation, then, is best understood as the realization and recognition of the *imago Dei* within the individual, and helping that individual utilize their gifts and talents in a way that contributes to the fabric of a restored virtuous community. Through that, we participate in the life of God. The practice of cultivating vocation is the practice of a community helping the individual recognizing their divinely offered gifts and helping them to understand those gifts through the lens of virtue. Through that, the community reorients itself to reflect its created intention.

CULTIVATING VOCATION IN THE SMALL CHURCH

Vocation is about both the individual and the community. Because the church is but one voice among many helping individuals understand who they are, reclaiming the work of cultivating vocation requires the church to reclaim its identity as a formational community. Otherwise, the myriad of voices render the narrative of vocation incoherent, limiting our ability to cultivate vocation intelligently. As MacIntyre points out, the competing claims of truthfulness, lacking any other telos, renders many of our important ethical and theological conversations unintelligible, because each individual can simply default to their preference, rather than appeal to something objective. Without some type of formational work, any conversation around vocation becomes muddled and meaningless.[21]

Accordingly, cultivating a deeper understanding of vocation requires a deeper telos, which in turn roots the individual in a community shaped by a common story—their narrative—and which are perpetuated by and contribute to a set of practices. As we explored in chapter 1, MacIntyre's threefold understanding of how to cultivate virtues serves to help the community move toward their ultimate telos. This movement toward the telos is the habit of virtue.[22]

Vocation, as we have described it here, is closely linked with that virtue. Cultivating vocation, then, requires us to cultivate habits of virtue. This means that the primary task of the local congregation is not just helping individuals uncover talents and finding ways to use them. Rather, it is about forming the individual within the narrative of the church and helping them utilize those talents in a way that points them toward their ultimate telos—the kingdom that is inaugurated through the resurrection of Jesus Christ.

Cultivating vocation becomes both a practice of evangelism and discipleship formation. It is evangelistic because it initiates individuals deeper into the kingdom of God. Both the individual and the congregation recognize the ways that their gifts and talents might be used to draw closer to God's work. It is discipleship because it awakens a new social and ethical reality, lived out by the people within the congregation because of their formation in the congregation. The understanding of vocation formed and shaped within the congregation stands in contrast to the notions of vocation shaped by the marketplace or the political arena. It invites a participation in the idea of the divine economy that Long references.

But vocation is not just abstract theology. Vocation is about the ways in which we live our lives, and as such, carries moral and ethical implications, both for the community and for the individual. By stunting vocational formation, a congregation can inhibit the discipleship of the community and limit the fullness of potential within their members.

Small-membership churches, fortunately, are well suited to embrace the work of forming vocations, because of the natural structures at work within them. Cultivating vocation requires three conditions that small churches hold in abundance. These three conditions— a strong sense of community, a clear story, and opportunities to practice—are inherent within the life of a small congregation.

Community

Vocation, like any other ethic or virtue, needs to be cultivated within a community. After all, humans are social. We need community. Theologian William Abraham notes that community is especially important for the formation of vocation, writing, "it is very difficult to see how Christians will be able to sustain the costly commitments that the gospel inaugurates without the nurture of a supportive social environment."[23] Christians must have a community to cultivate an appropriately focused understanding of vocation. Otherwise, their understanding of vocation will simply be defined by one of the many other spaces that seek to form and shape us, whether that is the marketplace, our friend groups, or some other social location.

When it comes to cultivating vocation, the community is formational in two specific ways. First, the community highlights and affirms the gifts and talents of the individual. Second, the community reorients those gifts toward the goal of the community. It is not enough to understand that an individual has gifts; the community must affirm that the gifts can be ordered toward the well-being of the community. Consider the narrative in Matthew 4:18–22 as a template. Jesus finds two fishermen and calls them by name, thus inviting them into a community. Jesus then identifies their particular talents, naming that they are fishermen. Finally, Jesus reorders that work toward the kingdom, inviting them to apply their talents to the kingdom of God.

As we've already seen, the small-membership church, at its core, is a place of community. Its relationality creates a place especially conducive to meaningful theological formation. As people join the community, they learn the habits, the language, and the ways of being together that shape them. A strong sense of community is inherently present in the small-membership church.

The Story

Cultivating any virtuous habit, including habits related to vocation, requires a formative story within which the community understands itself. Our story provides a framework for how decisions are made. As we understand the origins of our community, and the end that we hope for our community, we begin to think of our decisions and actions within that framework as well. Our framework for a decision becomes less of, "What do I want to do in this moment?" and more about, "What will help this story move forward?"

For the church, that story is the redemptive theological drama of God's work in the world. Sam Wells has helpfully illustrated this as a five-act play, following a narrative of Creation, Israel, Jesus, the Church, and the Eschaton.[24] When we realize that our community is part of that theodrama, we place ourselves in a larger narrative. We can even locate ourselves in a more specific portion of that play, Act IV: The Church. We are given freedom to improvise and act within that story. Our practices are able to join the unfolding narrative. As we act within that play, we remember the larger story, we respond to it, and we act in a way that drives the narrative forward.

Importantly, the story is both in the background and in the foreground, shaping the practice. It is more than a theoretical construct. It is influencing how we live and act. Or, as Bryan Stone puts it,

> The church's story is not a *theory* that can be applied in some direct way to practice. That relationship is instead a dynamic, historical, and intertextual process of community formation: the narrative is engaged imaginatively and assigned meaning by the community while at the same time overflowing into the community.[25]

The narrative of the community is essential because it allows people to understand the context in which they are acting. The narrative also enables the actors—the people that comprise a local congregation—to act faithfully. To root oneself in a story is to live in such a way that makes sense within the story.

This is necessary for cultivating vocation for three reasons. First, it gives meaning to what vocation can and should mean. In this case, as we have identified, it is aimed at initiation into the divine economy. Second, it provides boundaries by which the community and the individual can act, which, to borrow again from Sam Wells, provides opportunities for improvisation within the story, testing new gifts and new potential.[26] Third, it provides something to act toward. We are not only responding to what has come before but we are acting toward our telos. This acting toward our telos, as Stone tells us, is an act of hope.[27]

But this story can also be particularized and localized. Small congregations generally already have a strong sense of their community or neighborhood's history. They are keenly aware of familial histories and narratives, understanding how the congregation and the community have changed, though they may not always be able to come to terms with those changes. Small congregations are also well-equipped to identify challenges within their community and recount how those challenges continue to shape their realities.

It is a strength that small congregations already know their own community story. It allows them to overlay the story of their community and local church onto the theodrama that Sam Wells writes about. In doing so, they can better particularize their own location in the wider Christian narrative. The more a local church recognizes their story as interrelated with the Christian drama rather than as a separate drama, the more a local church can act in ways that bring the narratives into alignment. They can better recognize, for instance, a call for repentance, and see how they might grow as a community in the divine economy.

The community offers a place for others to name gifts and talents within an individual. The story of the community, the narrative, helps the community and the individual think through what it means to appropriately use those gifts. This becomes the foundation of vocation. People recognize their gifts and begin to better understand how it will help both them and their community move toward flourishing. But there is still another component that is necessary: the ability to practice as they grow in their vocation.

Opportunities to Practice

Theology and practice are intertwined. As Pohl writes, a focus on practice "allows us to see issues in congregational and community life from a different angle and helps us get at the moral and theological commitments that structure our relationships."[28] If a community has a story, it will require space to practice the habits that become formational.

William Abraham, in discussing the practices of spiritual disciplines, raises the stakes even further. Abraham rightly argues that spiritual disciplines nurture spiritual discernment. At the same time, spiritual disciplines sustain the individual in the "difficult commitments that both the beginning and the mature disciple have to face in the world as he or she seeks to live of a life of active love."[29] The ability to practice helps individuals and the communities know which decisions and habits will actually help them move toward flourishing, and which will pull them away from it.

Vocation, as a spiritual practice and discipline, requires spiritual discernment that runs counter to the prevailing narratives of other sectors of society. It too requires commitments that are difficult to keep. If a congregation is to affirm gifts and reorient an individual to use those gifts in a new story, they must provide a way for the individual to practice new skills, lest the individual be overwhelmed by the difficulty of imagining an alternative story without any template to follow.

Small-membership churches are especially well suited for this work. Within the small-membership church, a smaller staff necessitates more shared responsibility within the church. As we saw in earlier chapters, in the disorganized system that is a small-membership church, leaders might be potentially anyone who simply volunteers for a role.[30] Drawing on Barth, Lewis Parks argues that in small churches, church organization is a confessional act, "an intentional public witness in written form and practice that *this* community at *this* moment will order its life together *this* way in obedience to its Lord who summons."[31]

Within the small-membership church, the work of organizing the church itself becomes a useful arena for offering a place for members to practice their gifts within their new narrative. As we saw in the previous chapter, volunteers typically engage in small-membership churches in ways that support the ongoing life of the organization. The opportunities to practice new skills, shaped by the new narrative, take place in ordering the life and work of the church itself. The teenager can practice teaching a Sunday school class, deepening their understanding of teaching not just as content instruction but in facilitating curiosity and virtue. The owner of a convenient store can sit in Staff/Parish Relations Committee meetings or budget meetings, deepening their understanding of ethical leadership and business, or teaching others how values and business need not contradict. A contractor can use their skills to develop new missional opportunities in the community.

Importantly, the church also becomes a place to develop new skills, not just to reflect on existing ones. The small-membership church does not require a certain set of credentials to lead in a new area; in many cases, it simply requires showing up. A janitor might find that they are exceptionally talented at managing finances. An administrative assistant can develop skills in strategic planning and visioning. An accountant can practice preaching. A banker can become the liturgist. Within the small-membership church, there are ample opportunities for members to identify and practice their gifts in new and creative ways. In turn, the community helps the congregation recognize these vocational gifts as a way to live into the divine economy.

VOCATIONS ACROSS GENERATIONS

Vocation changes across time. Often, when I mention this, the immediate reaction is to relink vocation and work, and look at how people's jobs change over the course of a lifetime. As we have seen, though, always linking vocation to work can diminish the deeper truths about vocation and limit our potential for flourishing. It is not enough to say, "Of course someone's career choice will change over their lifetime." Instead, we need to recognize that vocation itself is about the flourishing of the individual and community. What it means to flourish is different at different points in our lives. When I was a child, flourishing meant learning to understand the world around me. In college, flourishing required establishing boundaries, learning to assert independence. As a parent and a husband in my midthirties, flourishing is much different. Now, my flourishing is tied to the flourishing of my children and the health of my marriage. My career is part of that, but it is only a part.

None of those things are realized alone, however. One gift of the small-membership church is in its ability to foster vocation at every stage of life. To illustrate that, let me paint three small portraits of people across generations and how the church might support their understanding of what it means to flourish.

The Vocation of the Child

Mackenzie is five years old. She is a big sister who recently moved from a small town to a city. Her parents got a new job, and so, in the middle of the year, she moved. Her new school is bigger. She has a different teacher. She struggles to remember names. Where she had a room to herself, she now shares a room with her little sister.

Like most five-year-olds, Mackenzie has a lot of what her dad calls "big emotions." She is excited to explore her new city. She loves not being alone at night and cherishes being in the same room as her sister. She is frustrated that she always has to share her toys. She misses her backyard. She misses her friends at her old school. She is overwhelmed. She is happy. She is sad. She is angry. She is thrilled. She yearns to prove that she is a capable big girl who can have more responsibilities and independence. She wants to be cuddled and feel safe by her parents. She wants to be left alone, and she wants attention.

Like learning a new school, Mackenzie has also learned a new church. Her new church is smaller than the one in her old, rural town. There are fewer kids, but Mackenzie isn't bothered by that. On Sunday mornings, Mackenzie goes to Sunday school and learns a Bible story. In regular school, Mackenzie has to watch how much she talks. In Sunday school, because there's just not a ton of kids, Mackenzie can ask questions and tell stories. She likes that she can listen to a Bible story and think about what it means. She likes to think about stories from her own life that relate to it. She confessed to the Sunday school teacher that one time, she didn't help her little sister like she should have when her little sister fell and scraped her knee. And she shared happily that she had given her sister one of her toys, even though it was her absolute favorite toy.

In "big church" Mackenzie strives to sit quietly. Sometimes, when she's feeling confident and brave, she goes up by herself for the children's time. Sometimes, she walks her sister up there. Sometimes, when she's feeling shy and scared, she asks her dad or her mom to sit with her. No one ever seems to mind.

Mackenzie feels safe at church. In a new city, where everything is bigger, the small church has been a safe harbor for her. Even though they haven't been there that long, the small number of people make her feel like she knows everyone. Sometimes, she asks the greeters if she can help pass out bulletins, and she finds her parents when she is done. Sometimes, she sits with her friends and waves to her parents across the sanctuary. She knows that if she wants to be a helper, she can be. If she needs reassurance, she will find it. When she has questions or needs someone to listen, she will find it there.

She is able to flourish, stretching her curiosity, discovering her limits, and practicing her emotions in a safe zone. She is teaching her parents to flourish as well. They are learning when to grant her independence, when to respect a boundary, when to grant her more responsibility, and when she needs to just be a kid. Through the life of the church, Mackenzie is teaching them to be parents. And the community is flourishing. Her Sunday school teacher, for instance, who had always wanted to teach but never thought they could, loves to watch Mackenzie make connections. Together, they are finding their vocation.

Middle-Aged Adults

At 54, Jeff is a father of three, a husband, and a human resources manager at a factory in his rural community. At a time when he thought things would calm down, Jeff is suddenly finding his life in chaos. His parents' health is rapidly declining, and he finds more and more of his week is spent on the phone with his siblings, trying to figure out the myriad questions that need to be answered at this stage of their lives. What do we do with their house? What do I do about their health? How do I help them navigate Medicare coverage?

Meanwhile, the constant in his life—his children—have now graduated and gone to college. Nightly check-ins about homework, school, the neverending volleyball matches and track meets have been traded out for a few ten-minute phone calls throughout the week and the occasional text message when the kids need help. His evenings, once a cacophony of teenage drama and family dinners, are no longer driven by his kids' schedule.

The pastor of his church approached him recently about serving on the Staff Parish Relations Committee. Since Jeff has a background in human resources, the pastor thought he might have experience to offer. Jeff agreed to do it, recognizing that he probably needed an outlet. And he recognized that he hadn't served on any committee or volunteered meaningfully in quite a while. Besides, the pastor told him, "It would be just like a normal HR team."

Except, Jeff realized quickly, it wasn't. Normal HR team meetings don't begin with a devotion and prayer, for starters. More than that, Jeff realized that the church's office policies need to be reworked. The church was small and only had one full-time staff person. But Jeff realized that there were areas of growth for the part-time employees.

After a few meetings, Jeff pointed this out. "We don't offer any sort of feedback to the part-time people. The nursery worker, the janitor, and the pianist."

"Sure," one his colleagues said, "But between the three of them, they're only getting paid $10,000. Why do we need to give them feedback?"

"What happens if we have to fire them?" Jeff said.

"We tell them they're fired. Come on Jeff. You're in HR. You fire people all the time."

"Right," Jeff said, "But there's always steps before that. Conversations, performance improvement plans, investigations. People are almost never surprised."

The committee sat in silence. Finally, the pastor spoke up. "Maybe we need a new policy. But if we make it, it needs to reflect who we are as a church. Not just a boilerplate HR policy from Walmart or something. I don't know how to do it. Jeff, could you help us lead it?"

Jeff agreed. First, he decided to meet with the pastor to talk more about what the pastor meant by "a policy that reflects the church." He and the pastor read through stories about work in the Bible. They talked about a theology of work. They looked at hard conversations in Scripture and thought deeply about how to balance the need to offer second chances, forgiveness, personal growth, and accountability. Pretty soon, Jeff decided that it wasn't really about performance reviews and firing. They were trying to create a staff policy to help every member of their staff flourish.

As he was working on the new policy, Jeff assembled a task force to help write it. One of the members, Sarah, was a lawyer in the community. Jeff didn't know what kind of law she practiced but thought it would be good to have a lawyer on the team. As they neared the conclusion of the policy revision process, Jeff made an appointment to look over the draft at Sarah's office.

Sarah found him pacing the sidewalk, on his phone. She didn't listen to much of his conversation, but she knew that Jeff sounded tense. When he came inside, she asked him if everything was OK.

"Yeah. You know. Aging parents. I think they're getting too old to live alone. But I don't know what to do about the power of attorney and health-care costs. It's complicated stuff."

"Jeff, you know I do geriatric law, right?" Sarah said. "I help people plan for this phase of life. Let's meet with your parents and look over their paperwork?"

"You gonna bill me for that, though."

"Well, let's start with a consultation. But then, yeah, you know us lawyers."

Several months later, the new staff policy at church was complete. As he presented it to the congregation at the quarterly business meeting, Jeff was surprised by how much he had enjoyed working on this new plan. He thought about faith and work in a new way, and it seeped into his work. He was still policy driven, but he was more sympathetic to employees who ended up in his office. Rather than drawing up performance improvement plans that were stepping stones to termination, Jeff started thinking through the plans as ways to really help the employee, even if they would be transitioning out. He added new components to annual reviews, too, ensuring that people got positive feedback on their evaluations.

Sarah had taken his parents on as clients. While it wasn't free, Sarah set up an easy payment plan and took much of the stress of planning his parent's end-of-life care off his shoulders. Jeff found himself focusing on enjoying the time with his parents rather than stressing about their medical and financial needs.

The church was strengthened, too. Through the process of reviewing the policy, the church took on new initiatives in mentorship and positive feedback. They added times to ensure they shared their gratitude with the part-time staff that often got ignored or worked in the background. A few of the Staff Parish Relations Committee members became mentors to the young nursery worker, a college student who had grown up in the church. As graduation approached, they ran practice interviews for her, to get used to job interviews. When she landed her first job, the committee threw a small celebration for her.

Recent Retirees

Susanna retired as an administrative assistant after thirty-two years, after her husband suddenly died of a heart attack. Her only daughter lived on the other side of the country. She felt alone, trapped in a suburban museum, surrounded by all the reasons they moved to this community. It was a quick commute to the office where she worked. Her daughter attended a great public school, and lots of her friends lived around them. But now, as a retired widow, she was surprised by how useless all of that was to her.

With the death of her husband, Susanna realized she didn't have a ton of friends around her. She was also tired of being a third wheel, joining other couples for dinner. She found herself hanging out at church more. Every Tuesday, she attended a Bible study. She liked it because it made her think. More than that, it gave her something to do.

One day, they talked about using their talents. The pastor asked them to think about how they could be leaders in the church and in the community. Susanna scoffed. "I am not a leader. I am a worker.

You tell me to do something, and I'll do it. But I'm not the one that's going to lead anything."

A few weeks later, before the pastor arrived, the Bible study group members were talking about how there used to be a senior citizen group in the church.

"I would love that," Susanna told the group. "I need something to do." The others agreed to bring it up to the pastor. The pastor liked the idea but told the group she couldn't lead it.

"I'm the only person on staff, and I've already got too much on my plate to organize that. If you can find someone to organize it, I'll make sure it has funding, and I'll join you all, though!"

Over the next few weeks, the Bible study members asked around to see if anyone would be willing to organize a group. Everyone loved the idea, but no one wanted the responsibility of leading it. Finally, Susanna had an idea. "Let's have a game day. We'll get some board games, cards, or dominoes. We'll just play games, and we can tap someone to lead the group there."

The game day was a success. Ten older adults, plus the pastor, sat in the fellowship hall playing dominoes. Susanna broached the conversation about who should be the leader of this group, but no one took the bait.

Disappointed that there would be no leader, Susanna tossed out a suggestion: "Well, I walk every Monday, Wednesday, and Friday at 9 a.m. over by the lake. Since we can't have a group, if anyone wants to join me, I guess they can."

The next Monday, three other seniors joined Susanna for a walk. Over the next few months, the number grew to an average of fifteen. Three days a week, the seniors went for a walk around the lake, talking about their lives, sharing their frustrations, and offering prayer requests to each other.

One day, as Bible study wrapped up, the pastor pointed to Susanna. "I want to say thanks for organizing the senior group. You've done a great job with that. I know a lot of people are really grateful for it."

"What? I didn't organize anything. I'm not a leader."

One of the other Bible study participants spoke up, "Well, you're the only reason we started. You're the one who sends out reminders. You're the one who keeps track of the prayers and checks on everyone. I think you're the leader."

Unexpectedly, Susanna found herself exercising a side of her vocation she never knew she had: leadership. Her small suburban church, through the lack of staff, gave her an opportunity to lead, even when she was convinced she couldn't. More than that, she offered a community to even more people. She was flourishing with a new vocation, and because of it, her church was flourishing too.

VOCATION IN THE SMALL CHURCH

In each of these stories, we see commonalities. The people are discovering vocation through the community around them. They are reminded of their stories. They are given chances to practice. It looks different for each one. For Mackenzie, she is learning her story by relating her life to that of the Bible stories she learns in Sunday school. The community gives her space to practice asking questions, space to practice new responsibilities, and space to be shy and confident all at once. For Jeff, the church helped him renarrate his work in the context of a smaller workforce, and it allowed him to find a support for a pressing need of his. As a result, the congregation moved from haphazardly employing part-time nursery workers to helping someone find a new job. Susanna found community again after losing her own narrative. She found that she was a leader, after all, and that she had an amazing talent for bringing people together. The church gave her a space to discover that talent, and through it, a whole group of people found a deeper connection.

The small-membership church is well positioned for these types of vocational exploration. It is the place where a group of people will tolerate the five-year-old handing out bulletins, wanting to play with her friends, or running back to her parents scared of being alone during the children's sermon. It is the place where a group of people come to care about the person who works only a few hours each week enough to help her prepare for a job. It is the place where a group of people can vulnerably and honestly share their hopes, frustrations, and losses as they walk around a lake together.

It happens in the small-membership church because cultivating vocation is ingrained in the vocation of what it means to be a small-membership church. At its very core, being a small-membership church is about being a community—a community with a story, a community with space for people to engage and work and belong. We don't always think of small-membership churches as flourishing, though we should. Yet, it is undeniable that these congregations are places where great flourishing can happen, where vocation is found in all its forms.

Conclusion

A myth of unfettered numerical growth as normative has taken root in our imaginations. Our economic worldview is saturated with the message that bigger means better. That same economic imagination, those same images of growth for the sake of growth, have saturated our ecclesial imagination as well so that when we consider words like *vitality* we are tempted to think of bigger.

I want to disrupt those images, to poke holes in the assumptions and myths that we carry through to small-membership churches. Over and over, from within these congregations and outside of them, I hear an echoed fear that small-membership churches are not enough, that they are not worthy or vital or successful. But these are vague terms with myriad meanings. Too often, we define these words through images and pictures. Images of vast programs, large budgets, churches teeming with people.

If we are to offer new definitions, then we need to offer new images. As the economist Kate Raworth reminds us, "we stand little chance of telling a new story if we stick to the old illustrations."[1] We cannot tell a story about the vibrant small-membership church if we have no illustrations to gesture toward. We cannot talk about the vocation of the small-membership church if our only example of thriving congregations are ones based on larger organizational models that offer different ways of living out their theologies and different ways of engaging and interacting. Rather, to tell stories about how powerful small congregations can be, we need meaningful illustrations about the importance of "small" in the kingdom of God.

Scripture does good work of this for us. Consider two parables in which small things are the moral and spiritual focus of the story: the Parable of the Mustard Seed and the Parable of the Leaven. In Matthew and Luke, these parables are lumped together.[2] In the first, Jesus likens the kingdom of Heaven to a mustard seed. It is a small seed that grows wildly and quickly. In the second parable, the kingdom of Heaven adds a bit of leaven to bread, which results in a huge amount of bread.

I suspect that we often interpret these parables as offering pictures of unfettered growth. We might be tempted to focus on the end result of these stories. Great things are done; big changes are made. After all, the small mustard seed produces a persistent shrub; the leaven produces a large yield of bread.

But the point of these stories is not that small things become big things. If that were the point, Jesus could have easily referenced the height and strength of the cedar trees of Lebanon, drawing deep from the well of Old Testament symbols.[3] Instead, the emphasis is on the large change that something small brought about.

New Testament scholar R. T. France notes that these parables remind us that "the Kingdom of God may be initially insignificant, but it is pervasive."[4] So, our work of discipleship is not being the mustard tree or being the large basket of bread. Rather, discipleship is about being the small, pervasive, world-changing item. We do not know the effects or repercussions of our ministry by small congregations. We only know that in being the leaven or the mustard seed, we can live toward our telos. At their core, these parables are about the mysterious outcomes of what can feel insignificant, even though the seemingly insignificant are agents of the kingdom of God. These parables are poignant illustrations of the impact of small. What is seen as insignificant is powerful. What is seen as small brings about great change.

The illustration of unfettered numerical growth, in reality, is not one that is particularly helpful to small-membership churches. It is an image that confuses our telos, which in turn confuses our practices and discipleship. Rather than being the leaven or the mustard seed, we focus on becoming the mustard tree or the basket of bread. When our images of what it means to be vital or successful are largely based on not being a small-membership church, we lose what makes our small congregations beautiful places of God's mission.

Small-membership churches have a missional purpose, and they have the capacity to live into their vocation and mission. In order to do that, as we have explored, they must learn to use those tools with which they are naturally equipped. Their relational organizations make them perfect for life-altering ministry in their communities. At the same time, they must embrace an image of being missional that aligns with the skills and gifts of their congregations.

So, what does this ministry look like? There are countless examples of the small-membership church in deep ministry and mission to their communities. I want to share the work of two churches that have different types of leaders and serve in different contexts. One is rural; one is urban. One is considered more conservative; one is more progressive. While these two churches' stories are not inclusive of all the diversity of small-membership churches, I hope they offer a glimpse into how a small-membership church might live into its vocation of being small.

ELKTON METHODIST CHURCH

Elkton Methodist Church is a landmark in its small Tennessee town. Located about five miles from the Alabama border, the church is housed in a historic brick building with grand columns, just off the main road. It is frequently used as a reference point for drivers passing through the town of Elkton, which has fewer than six hundred residents.

"People all know where the church is. It's how you give directions," says their pastor, Reverend Brad Smith. I got to know Smith through my previous role at a small college a few miles north of his town.

When my center supported a cohort to help rural congregations develop community change programs, Smith became a vital cohort member and a conversation partner for my center's work in the community.

A native of the community, Smith has served for nearly a decade as the congregation's pastor. The church boasts an average worship attendance of around twenty-five. Despite its small size, Smith is keenly aware of the outsized presence the congregation has in the community. "There are three institutions in this town. There's the post office. There's the school. There's the church. If one of those was to close, the community would collapse."

For Smith and his congregation, part of the church's role is to act as a social safety net for the members of their community. Some of that protection happens through participating in cooperative programs like the Community Rural Food Delivery. Once a month, volunteers distribute hundreds of boxes of food for families within the county, frequently running out of food. Similarly, the church collects school supplies for their local school, which has about three hundred students ranging from kindergarten to eighth grade. In 2021, the small congregation donated close to $1,200 in supplies.

More frequently, though, the congregation simply responds to whatever need arises. In the early days of the COVID-19 pandemic, Smith watched as rural schools and churches began migrating to virtual meetings. Since he became the pastor of Elkton United Methodist Church eight years ago, Smith had been trying to convince his own congregation to install Wi-Fi in the church building. As the pandemic forced people online, he saw a chance to solve two problems. The church had a large amount of funds set aside for church growth initiatives without clear instructions on how that money should be utilized. Smith noted that the church wanted to be intentional about using those funds appropriately. "How do you measure that? Can it just be for outreach?" he recalled, of the conversations.

Then, the regional leadership of Smith's denomination put restrictions on in-person gathering. Smith began convincing church leaders that providing Internet access in the church was a necessity, telling them, "Look, if we're going to livestream the worship service, we have to have Internet." After some conversation, the congregation secured Internet access and added Wi-Fi capabilities.

With the necessary technology in place, Smith began looking for more possibilities to support the community during the pandemic. "I read an article . . . where they were using buses, parked in strategic areas, to give kids access to the internet. And I thought, why can't the church do that? We're right here." Soon after, the church shared that anyone needing to use their Wi-Fi could access it free of charge from the church parking lot. "We might only get one or two people needing it at a time, but that's one or two people that, if we weren't here, wouldn't have it," says Smith, comparing it to the storm shelter run in the basement of the church. "It doesn't really cost us anything. Sometimes no one comes. Sometimes we get one person who really needs it. But without us, what would they do?"

Because the church doesn't have staff or program volunteers, Smith notes that the congregation focuses on providing quick responses to the needs that arise within the community. "When you have a need, you can't wait a month or two for a committee to meet and make a decision." The congregation's willingness to meet immediate needs in the community is part of the reason the church is so integral to the life of the town. Or, as Smith once told me, "If this church were to close, people wouldn't have a meeting place. People would fall through the cracks. It would be part of the story of decline for this community."

FIRST UNITED METHODIST CHURCH OF SANFORD

Sanford, Florida is located just outside of Orlando.[5] It is a bustling and growing metropolitan area close to Disney World and not too far from the incredibly busy Orlando airport, a community rapidly being changed by an influx of people into the region. In 2012, Sanford became synonymous with the homicide of Trayvon Martin, a seventeen-year-old African American boy. In many ways, Sanford is a community of paradox. Wealth and poverty mingle. New growth and old traditions battle. Like in most places, racism is hidden but always present.

Since 1915, First United Methodist Church has occupied its current structure. Currently, the church averages around ninety, a significant decline from nearly twenty years ago when it was firmly a midsized congregation with around two hundred in average worship attendance. As the community grew, so did the number of megachurches in the region. To compete with that growth, First United would need to alter its DNA. More than that, the congregation would need to abandon its physical place in the community—rapid growth would not be possible on the city block it occupied.

Meghan and David Killingsworth were appointed copastors of this congregation in 2017. Rather than push the congregation toward adding new members, Meghan began an intentional conversation around what she describes as missional metrics. Her questions focused more on the assets of the church: What are the needs we can meet? How might we be incarnational within our community? What does it mean to be a leader in this particular community? Where do we fit in the current ecosystem?

For their congregation, one of the clear answers to this question was a conversation about better utilizing its building. The congregation began a plan to launch a coworking and incubator space for nonprofits in the community. Eventually, this venture became The Neighborhood Co-Op. The space is open to 501(c)3 organizations in the community and small businesses who have missions to invest in the flourishing of the whole community. As part of their partnership, all of the co-op members gather for shared training and have partner networks to aid in grant applications. Today, the co-op boasts seven organizations in the shared space.

Remarkably, the First UMC branding and logo is nowhere to be found on the co-op's website. The only clue that the co-op is affiliated with a church is the address, which shares the same red brick as the church it grew from. The co-op is a mustard tree grown out of a mustard seed.

THE GIFT OF SMALL

What I prize and admire about these two congregations is their commitment to being true to their vocations. They do not lament their average worship attendance. Rather, they embrace who they are and allow their identities to shape how they live out their missions. In Elkton, the church is a hallmark of the community, a safety net that will catch the people who need it the most. Its congregation members are the ones who keep an ear to the ground, willing and able to respond quickly as a need arises. In Sanford, the church is a congregation that uses its connections in the community to do great things, even if it means leaving the safety and comfort of organizational ownership. Its congregation members are content to release the outcome to God. They are patient enough to see that God can use them because of who they are.

Small-membership churches are places of deep potential, but it is not necessarily the potential to be bigger. It is not always the potential to have more programs or to get a larger budget. It is the potential to grow the kingdom of God in delightfully surprising new ways. It is the potential to shape the lives of individuals and community members through deep relationships. It is the potential to offer a vocation to others.

Our small-membership churches need not apologize for being small. Rather, our small-membership churches can and should embrace their gifts. They should embrace their vocations. They should embrace those realities that make them who they are. In doing so, our small-membership churches will recognize that being small is not a lament at all. It is a great gift for the kingdom of God.

Notes

INTRODUCTION

1 See, for instance, William H. Willimon, *Accidental Preacher: A Memoir* (Grand Rapids, MI: Eerdmans, 2019), 204.
2 William J. Abraham, *The Logic of Evangelism* (Grand Rapids, MI: Eerdmans, 1989), 102–103.

CHAPTER ONE

1 Romans 12:2, 9–21.
2 James 2:17.
3 William J. Abraham, *The Logic of Evangelism* (Grand Rapids, MI: Eerdmans, 1989), 143.
4 Abraham, *Logic of Evangelism*, 135.
5 John E. Senior, *A Theology of Political Vocation: Christian Life and Public Office* (Waco, TX: Baylor University Press, 2015), 49–50.
6 Kate Raworth, *Doughnut Economics: Seven Ways to Think Like a 21st Century Economist* (White River Junction, VT: Chelsea Green Publishing, 2017), 19.
7 Cynthia M. Duncan, *Worlds Apart: Poverty and Politics in Rural America*, 2nd ed. (New Haven, CT: Yale University Press, 2014), 235–236.
8 D. Stephen Long, *Divine Economy: Theology and the Market* (London: Routledge, 2000), 6.
9 Long, *Divine Economy*, 61.
10 Raworth, *Doughnut Economics*, 28.
11 Raworth, *Doughnut Economics*, 29.
12 Raworth, *Doughnut Economics*, 21.
13 Matthew 28:18–20.
14 Mortimer Arias, "'The Great Commission': Mission as Discipleship," *Journal of the Academy for Evangelism in Theological Education* 4 (1988): 23–24.
15 Arias, "The Great Commission," 17.
16 Arias, "The Great Commission," 22.

17 Arias, "The Great Commission," 22.

18 Mitzi J. Smith, "'Knowing More than Is Good for One': A Womanist Interrogation of the Matthean Great Commission," in *Teaching All Nations: Interrogating the Matthean Great Commission*, ed. Mitzi J. Smith and Jayachitra Lalitha (Minneapolis: Fortress Press, 2014), 135.

19 Anthony G. Reddie, "Beginning Again: Rethinking Christian Education in Light of the Great Commission," in *Teaching All Nations: Interrogating the Matthean Great Commission* (Minneapolis: Fortress Press, 2014), 245.

20 Bryan P. Stone, *Evangelism after Christendom: The Theology and Practice of Christian Witness* (Grand Rapids, MI: Brazos Press, 2007), 15.

21 Alasdair C. MacIntyre, *After Virtue: A Study in Moral Theory*, 3rd ed. (Notre Dame, IN: University of Notre Dame Press, 2007), 148.

22 MacIntyre, *After Virtue*, 144.

23 MacIntyre, *After Virtue*, 221.

24 MacIntyre, *After Virtue*, 187.

25 MacIntyre, *After Virtue*, 187.

26 Brad Kallenberg, "The Master Argument of MacIntyre's After Virtue," in *Virtues and Practices in the Christian Tradition: Christian Ethics after MacIntyre*, ed. Nancy Murphy, Brad Kallenberg, and Mark Nation (Harrisburg, PA: Trinity Press International, 1997), 20.

27 Arias, "'The Great Commission': Mission as Discipleship," 22.

28 Christine D. Pohl, *Living into Community: Cultivating Practices That Sustain Us* (Grand Rapids, MI: Eerdmans, 2012), 165.

29 Pohl, *Living into Community*, 165–167.

30 For a deeper exploration of the Church Growth Movement, especially its relationship to the Civil Rights Movement, see Jesse Curtis, "White Evangelicals as a 'People': The Church Growth Movement from India to the United States," *Religion and American Culture* 30, no. 1 (2020): 108–146, https://doi.org/10.1017/rac.2020.2. For a deeper exploration on evangelism and the Church Growth Movement, see Priscilla Pope Levison's *Models of Evangelism* (Grand Rapids, MI: Baker Academic, 2020).

31 Priscilla Pope-Levison, *Models of Evangelism* (Grand Rapids, MI: Baker Academic, 2020), 91–92.

32 Pope-Levison, *Models of Evangelism*, 92. Emphasis original.

33 Pope-Levison, *Models of Evangelism*, 110.

34 Pope-Levison, *Models of Evangelism*, 101.

35 Curtis, "White Evangelicals as a 'People,'" 122.

36 Curtis, "White Evangelicals as a 'People,'" 130.

37 Curtis, "White Evangelicals as a 'People,'" 132.

38 Tod E. Bolsinger, *Canoeing the Mountains: Christian Leadership in Uncharted Territory*, Expanded Edition (Downers Grove, IL: IVP Books, 2018), 96.

39 Bolsinger, *Canoeing the Mountains*, 90–94.

40 Bolsinger, *Canoeing the Mountains*, 214.
41 Bolsinger, *Canoeing the Mountains*, 18.
42 Ronald A. Heifetz, Alexander Grashow, and Martin Linsky, *The Practice of Adaptive Leadership: Tools and Tactics for Changing Your Organization and the World* (Boston: Harvard Business Press, 2009), 118–119.
43 Stone, *Evangelism after Christendom*, 272.
44 Bolsinger, *Canoeing the Mountains*, 90–94.
45 Richard H. Thaler and Cass R. Sunstein, *Nudge: Improving Decisions about Health, Wealth, and Happiness*, rev. and expanded ed. (New York: Penguin Books, 2009), 85.
46 Thaler and Sunstein, *Nudge: Improving Decisions about Health, Wealth, and Happiness*, 85.
47 Stone, *Evangelism after Christendom*, 170.
48 Pohl, *Living into Community*, 4.
49 Carl S. Dudley, *Effective Small Churches in the Twenty-First Century*, rev. and updated ed. (Nashville, TN: Abingdon Press, 2003), 40.
50 J. Rappaport, "Community Narratives: Tales of Terror and Joy," *American Journal of Community Psychology* 28, no. 1 (2000): 4–5.
51 Rappaport, "Community Narratives," 5.
52 Dudley, *Effective Small Churches*, 40.
53 John P. Kotter, "Capturing the Opportunities and Avoiding the Threats of Rapid Change," *Leader to Leader* 2014, no. 74 (September 2014): 32–37, https://doi.org/10.1002/ltl.20150. Kotter outlines the differences between leaner start-up organizations and established large organizations. As organizations grow larger, they add hierarchical layers, which limits the flow of information. A key trait of smaller, leaner organization is the rapid dissemination of information.
54 Stone, *Evangelism after Christendom*, 202.
55 Dudley, *Effective Small Churches*, 103.
56 Dudley, *Effective Small Churches*, 58–59.

CHAPTER TWO

1 William H. Willimon, *Pastor: The Theology and Practice of Ordained Ministry* (Nashville, TN: Abingdon Press, 2002), 60.
2 Willimon, *Pastor*, 60–61.
3 Carey Nieuwhof, "Pastoral Care for Healthy Churches (and Pastors)," *Carey Nieuwhof* (blog), n.d.
4 "How Pastoral Care Stunts the Growth of Most Churches," CareyNieuwhof.com, November 16, 2015, https://tinyurl.com/8dts2rpp.
5 Carl S. Dudley, *Effective Small Churches in the Twenty-First Century*, rev. and updated ed (Nashville, TN: Abingdon Press, 2003), 48.

6   Dudley, *Effective Small Churches*, 81.
7   Dudley, *Effective Small Churches*, 83.
8   Daniel Kahneman, *Thinking, Fast and Slow*, 1st pub. ed. (New York: Farrar, Straus and Giroux, 2013), 411.
9   Daniel Kahneman, Olivier Sibony, and Cass R. Sunstein, *Noise: A Flaw in Human Judgment* (New York: Little, Brown, 2021), 28–29.
10 Margaret M. Hopkins and Robert D. Yonker, "Managing Conflict with Emotional Intelligence: Abilities That Make a Difference," *Journal of Management Development* 34, no. 2 (March 2, 2015): 227, https://doi.org/10.1108/JMD-04-2013-0051.
11 Hopkins and Yonker, "Managing Conflict with Emotional Intelligence," 227.

CHAPTER THREE

1   Daniel Kahneman, Olivier Sibony, and Cass R. Sunstein, *Noise: A Flaw in Human Judgment* (New York: Little, Brown, 2021), 25–26.
2   Richard H. Thaler and Cass R. Sunstein, *Nudge: Improving Decisions about Health, Wealth, and Happiness*, rev. and expanded ed. (New York: Penguin Books, 2009), 85.
3   John P. Kotter, "Capturing the Opportunities and Avoiding the Threats of Rapid Change," *Leader to Leader* 2014, no. 74 (September 2014): 33, https://doi.org/10.1002/ltl.20150.
4   Kotter, "Capturing the Opportunities," 33.
5   Kotter, "Capturing the Opportunities," 34.
6   Kotter, "Capturing the Opportunities," 35–37.
7   James C. Collins, *Good to Great: Why Some Companies Make the Leap—and Others Don't* (New York: HarperBusiness, 2001), 94–97.
8   William Bridges, "Managing Organizational Transitions," *Organizational Dynamics* 15, no. 1 (1986): 24–33,
9   William Bridges, "Getting Them Through the Wilderness," William Bridges Associates, accessed May 2, 2022, https://tinyurl.com/53bbewt9.
10 Bridges, "Managing Organizational Transitions," 27–31.
11 Bridges, "Getting Them Through the Wilderness."
12 Lisa G. Fischbeck, "The Strength and Beauty of Small Churches," Faith and Leadership, accessed May 2, 2022, https://tinyurl.com/4unz3r55.
13 Nathan O. Hatch, "The Puzzle of American Methodism," *Church History* 63, no. 2 (June 1994): 178–179, https://doi.org/10.2307/3168586.
14 Harley Atkinson and Joel Comiskey, "Lessons from the Early House Church for Today's Cell Groups," *Christian Education Journal* 11, no. 1 (2014): 78.
15 Atkinson and Comiskey, 80.

CHAPTER FOUR

1 Mark Chaves et al., "Congregations in 21st Century America." (Durham, NC: Duke University, Department of Sociology, 2021), 4.

2 Chaves et al., "Congregations in 21st Century America," 10.

3 These figures are based on statistics available at www.umdata.com, which is maintained by the General Council on Finance and Administration for the United Methodist Church.

4 Chaves et al., "Congregations in 21st Century America," 10.

5 These figures are based on statistics available through the National Congregations Survey, available at https://tinyurl.com/4nuys4cz.

6 Chaves et al., "Congregations in 21st Century America.," 12.

7 Mareike Ernst et al., "Loneliness before and during the COVID-19 Pandemic: A Systematic Review with Meta-Analysis," *American Psychologist*, May 9, 2022, 2, https://doi.org/10.1037/amp0001005.

8 Ernst et al., "Loneliness before and during the COVID-19 Pandemic," 12.

9 Pope-Levison, *Models of Evangelism*, 39.

10 Pope-Levison, *Models of Evangelism*, 46.

11 "About Fresh Expressions," Fresh Expressions, accessed July 5, 2022, https://freshexpressions.com/about.

12 Carl S. Dudley, *Effective Small Churches in the Twenty-First Century*, rev. and updated ed. (Nashville, TN: Abingdon Press, 2003), 45.

13 Dudley, *Effective Small Churches*, 43.

14 Dudley, *Effective Small Churches*, 47.

15 Chaves et al., "Congregations in 21st Century America," 10.

16 Lewis Parks, *Small on Purpose: Life in a Significant Church* (Nashville, TN: Abingdon Press, 2017), 52.

17 Dudley, *Effective Small Churches*, 55.

CHAPTER FIVE

1 Mark Chaves et al., "Congregations in 21st Century America." (Durham, NC: Duke University, Department of Sociology, 2021), 42.

2 These figures are based on statistics available through the National Congregations Survey, available at https://tinyurl.com/tcr7dut6.

3 Judith Ann Trolander, *From Sun Cities to the Villages* (University Press of Florida, 2011), 250–251, https://doi.org/10.5744/florida/9780813036045.001.0001.

4 Nick Paumgarten, "Retirement the Margaritaville Way," *New Yorker*, March 21, 2022, https://tinyurl.com/yvvc6pvv.

5 Caroline Tremblay, "Radically Rural: Turning the Silver Tsunami into Gold," *The Daily Yonder*, January 6, 2020, https://tinyurl.com/svp2pvbh.

6 Kathleen A. Cahalan and Bonnie Miller-McLemore, eds., "Late Adulthood," in *Calling All Years Good: Christian Vocation throughout Life's Seasons* (Grand Rapids, MI: Eerdmans, 2017), 158.

7 Cahalan and Miller-McLemore, "Late Adulthood," 160.

8 Cahalan and Miller-McLemore, "Late Adulthood," 162.

9 Cahalan and Miller-McLemore, "Late Adulthood," 163.

10 Karl Barth, Geoffrey William Bromiley, Thomas F. Torrance, Rudolf J. Ehrlich, and Hendrickson Publishers, *The Doctrine of Creation*, Volume 3, Part 4 (Peabody, MA: Hendrickson Publishers, 2010), 537.

11 Barth, Ehrlich, and Hendrickson Publishers, 539–540.

12 Kathleen A. Cahalan and Bonnie Miller-McLemore, eds., "Older Adulthood," in *Calling All Years Good: Christian Vocation throughout Life's Seasons* (Grand Rapids, MI: Eerdmans, 2017), 181.

13 Cahalan and Miller-McLemore, "Older Adulthood," 183.

14 Cahalan and Miller-McLemore, "Older Adulthood," 186.

CHAPTER SIX

1 "Call to Action: Steering Team Report" (Nashville, TN: The United Methodist Church, 2010), 44, umc.org/calltoaction.

2 Mark Chaves et al., "Congregations in 21st Century America." (Durham, NC: Duke University, Department of Sociology, 2021), 12.

3 Lesley Hustinx, Debbie Haski-Leventhal, and Femida Handy, "One of a Kind? Comparing Episodic and Regular Volunteers at the Philadelphia Ronald McDonald House," *The International Journal of Volunteer Administration* XXV, no. 3 (November 2008): 62.

4 Hustinx, Haski-Leventhal, and Handy, "One of a Kind?" 62.

5 Hustinx, Haski-Leventhal, and Handy, "One of a Kind?" 62.

6 Hustinx, Haski-Leventhal, and Handy, "One of a Kind?" 62.

7 Chaves et al., "Congregations in 21st Century America," 15.

8 Hustinx, Haski-Leventhal, and Handy, "One of a Kind?" 57.

9 Hustinx, Haski-Leventhal, and Handy, "One of a Kind?" 62.

10 Hustinx, Haski-Leventhal, and Handy, "One of a Kind?" 57.

11 "2019 Clergy Health Initiative Summary Report: 2019 Statewide Survey of United Methodist Clergy in North Carolina" (Duke Divinity School, 2019), https://tinyurl.com/yt8sv3ve.

CHAPTER SEVEN

1 Sandra Beardsall, "A Funny Thing Happened . . . 'Vocation' in the Reformation Era," *Touchstone* 34, no. 2 (2016): 9.

2 Beardsall, "A Funny Thing Happened," 11.

3 Beardsall, "A Funny Thing Happened," 11.
4 Beardsall, "A Funny Thing Happened," 11.
5 Karl Barth, Geoffrey William Bromiley, Thomas F. Torrance, Rudolf J. Ehrlich, and Hendrickson Publishers, *The Doctrine of Creation, Volume III, Part 4* (Peabody, MA: Hendrickson Publishers, 2010), 538.
6 Barth, Ehrlich, and Hendrickson Publishers, 538.
7 Barth, Ehrlich, and Hendrickson Publishers, 539–540.
8 Thomas Wells and Johan Graafland, "Adam Smith's Bourgeois Virtues in Competition," *Business Ethics Quarterly* 22, no. 2 (April 2012): 325, https://doi.org/10.5840/beq201222222.
9 Wells and Graafland, 101.
10 Wells and Graafland, 101.
11 Steven Garber, *Visions of Vocation: Common Grace for the Common Good* (Downers Grove, IL: IVP Books, 2014), 80.
12 Garber, *Visions of Vocation*, 17, 135.
13 Garber, *Visions of Vocation*, 18.
14 Garber, *Visions of Vocation*, 135–170.
15 Katherine Turpin, "Younger Adulthood: Exploring Calls in the Midst of Uncertainty," in *Calling All Years Good: Christian Vocation throughout Life's Seasons*, ed. Kathleen A. Cahalan and Bonnie Miller-McLemore (Grand Rapids, MI: Eerdmans, 2017), 98.
16 Kathleen A. Cahalan, "Callings Over a Lifetime: In Relationship, through the Body, over Time, and for Community," in *Calling All Years Good: Christian Vocation throughout Life's Seasons*, ed. Kathleen A. Cahalan and Bonnie Miller-McLemore (Grand Rapids, MI: Eerdmans, 2017), 14–15.
17 D. Stephen Long, *Divine Economy: Theology and the Market* (London: Routledge, 2000), 230.
18 Long, *Divine Economy*, 236.
19 Long, *Divine Economy*, 236.
20 Long, *Divine Economy*, 268.
21 Alasdair C. MacIntyre, *After Virtue: A Study in Moral Theory*, 3rd ed. (Notre Dame, IN: University of Notre Dame Press, 2007), 20–22.
22 MacIntyre, *After Virtue*, 223.
23 William J. Abraham, *The Logic of Evangelism* (Grand Rapids, MI: Eerdmans, 1989), 195.
24 Samuel Wells, *Improvisation: The Drama of Christian Ethics* (Grand Rapids, MI: Brazos Press, 2018), 53.
25 Bryan P. Stone, *Evangelism after Christendom: The Theology and Practice of Christian Witness* (Grand Rapids, MI: Brazos Press, 2007), 172.
26 Wells, *Improvisation*, 78–84.
27 Stone, *Evangelism after Christendom*, 56.
28 Christine D. Pohl, *Living into Community: Cultivating Practices That Sustain Us* (Grand Rapids, MI: Eerdmans, 2012), 5.
29 Abraham, *The Logic of Evangelism*, 162.

30 Lewis Parks, *Small on Purpose: Life in a Significant Church* (Nashville, TN: Abingdon Press, 2017), 76.
31 Parks, *Small on Purpose*, 72.

CONCLUSION

1 Raworth, *Doughnut Economics*, 11.
2 The Parable of the Mustard Seed also appears in Mark's gospel (4:30–32).
3 Green, *The Gospel of Luke*, 527.
4 France, *The Gospel of Matthew*, 528.
5 Parts of this section are drawn from an essay I originally wrote for *Faith and Leadership* (www.faithandleadership.com). That essay can be found at https://faithandleadership.com/allen-t-stanton-rural-churches-can-thrive-beyond-numbers.